Community Action Groups and City Governments

Community Action Groups and City Governments

Perspectives from
Ten American Cities

Frank X. Steggert

Ballinger Publishing Company • Cambridge, Mass.
A Subsidiary of J.B. Lippincott Company

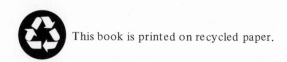 This book is printed on recycled paper.

International Standard Book Number: 0-88410-415-X

Library of Congress Catalog Card Number: 75-5912

Printed in the United States of America

Library of Congress Cataloging in Publication Data

Steggert, Frank X
    Community action groups and city governments.
    Includes bibliographies.
    1. Citizens' associations—United States. 2. Municipal government—United States. 3. Political participation—United States. I. Title.
JS303.5.S73   352'.008   75-5912
ISBN 0-88410-415-X

Contents

List of Tables and Figures

Figures

Preface

The research forming the basis for this book was conducted under a contract between the National League of Cities and the U.S. Department of Housing and Urban Development. The substance of the research is dedicated to the public. The original report was prepared for the Department of Housing and Urban Development under its contract with the National League of Cities.

The book draws from material presented in the final reports of ten participating Urban Observatories. (These studies are listed in Appendix B.) Findings from individual cities have been used for explanatory or illustrative purposes. These citations should not be viewed as summaries of the individual city studies. In order to have any adequate sense of what was studied in each city, individual reports should be consulted. The treatments of study materials and interpretations of outcomes are, therefore, the sole responsibility of the author. Many city study directors have, however, reacted to an earlier draft of this book. Those who responded evidenced basic agreement with the author's analysis of data and primary conclusions. The author is, of course, responsible for any errors or omissions that remain.

I am grateful to the many researchers and officials in Urban Observatory cities who contributed to the citizen participation project. Special thanks are due Lawrence A. Williams of the National League of Cities for his continuous support, assistance and encouragement throughout the project; and Floyd J. Fowler, Jr., of the University of Massachusetts at Boston, for his assistance in obtaining data from the Urban Observatory Program's Citizens' Attitude Survey.

Introduction

The essential findings of the Urban Observatory Program's[1] study of organized citizen participation are summarized in this book. It is my distillation of a large body of material stemming from cooperative research under the auspices of ten different Urban Observatories.

The cities cooperating in the study were Albuquerque; Atlanta, Baltimore; Boston; Cleveland; Denver; Kansas City, Kansas; Kansas City, Missouri; Milwaukee; Nashville; and San Diego. The two Kansas Cities are served by the same Observatory, and thus all ten research centers in the original Urban Observatory Program participated in this network-wide citizen participation study.[2] Each prepared a final report.[3]

No attempt has been made to include all the findings of the different reports. Although the studies had common starting points and used similar methods, they also reflected the particular concerns of officials and researchers in individual study cities. The additional studies in Boston (of the Little City Hall program) and in Denver (of Model Cities and other programs) illustrate such special local interests. In other cities, certain aspects of citizen participation were probed in greater-than-usual depth.[4]

The overall result of the ten-city study is a body of rich material—findings, concepts, and speculations—about organized citizen participation in urban areas. In order to provide some flavor of what certain parts of the individual city studies were all about, a series of statements appears in Appendix B.[5] These brief fragments should *not* be viewed as summaries of the studies. In order to have any adequate sense of what was studied in Albuquerque or Nashville or any other participating city, individual final reports should be consulted (these are listed in Appendix B).

This book's emphasis, therefore, is on common findings—

areas where a number of reports have produced similar or complementing results. Within this context, information from a single city is used for explanatory or illustrative purposes. Common findings are reported under three general headings: (1) the kinds of citizen groups engaged in contacts with city governments; (2) the issues that triggered such involvements; and (3) estimates of group effectiveness.

Another study of the Urban Observatory Program—the Citizens' Attitude Survey[6]—provided directly comparable information about some aspects of organizational membership in citizen participation study cities. Significant findings from these data provide an appropriate frame of reference for the study of organized citizen participation. These background findings are summarized in Chapter 2.

The Urban Observatory Program's study of organized citizen participation represents, in one sense, the first systematic study of community action groups and their relationships with local governments. Thus this book is one of the few works in the citizen participation and community involvement literature that stems from a group of original research efforts. Since it draws from a cooperative multi-city research activity, its conclusions go beyond the more limited results of traditional single-city case studies.

This book's coverage is also broader than most other citizen participation inquiries. It focuses on all major categories of activist community groups. It deals with groups brought into being by federal urban programs of the sixties, more conventional citizen organizations created by direct actions of local governments, and voluntary bodies organized by local special interest groups. A final section examines current relationships of organized citizen action to the local political system and its community planning and development processes. During an era of ongoing decentralization and with federal revenue-sharing's emphasis on local responsibility, this is an increasingly important consideration.

NOTES

1. For a recent description of the Urban Observatory Program and its general character and objectives, see Lawrence A. Williams, "The Urban Observatory Program," a special report segment in the December 1974 issue of *Nation's Cities*. See also the sequence of articles by Lawrence A. Williams, William P. Irwin, Victor Jones, and Marshall E. Dimmock (together with associated material) in the September 1972 issue of the *Urban Affairs Quarterly*. For an earlier perspective,

see Frank X. Steggert, "Urban Observatories: An Experiment in Institution Building," paper presented at the 1969 National Conference of the American Society for Public Administration, Miami Beach, Florida. For an academic assessment, see F. William Heiss, *Urban Research and Urban Policy-Making: An Observatory Approach* (Bureau of Governmental Research, University of Colorado, Boulder, 1974).

2. With eleven cities and ten urban observatories involved, it is a moot question whether the total enterprise should be referred to as involving a ten-city or an eleven-city study. Since the Urban Observatory Program has been thought of as a ten-city network, and for purposes of consistency, this report will refer to the ten-city study. As will be noted later, the study in Cleveland was not city-wide in its focus.

3. See Appendix B for a description of national agenda, local option, and associated studies under the auspices of the Urban Observatory Program.

4. See Appendix B.

5. These are highlights that have been pulled out and edited for purposes of this book. Paragraph-long summaries have been deliberately sequenced to fit into an overall summary statement. More orthodox summaries appear in those final reports available from the National Technical Information Service.

6. An initial summary of the findings of the Citizens' Attitude Survey appeared in a special report segment of the August and November 1971 issues of *Nation's Cities,* a recurring publication of the National League of Cities. A consolidation of these two articles was published by the National League of Cities as a *Nation's Cities* special report in November 1971. A full report of this project was published in 1974 by the Ballinger Publishing Company of Cambridge, Massachusetts. The title of this book by Floyd J. Fowler, Jr. is *Citizen Attitudes toward Local Government, Services, and Taxes.* As this title suggests, survey results have no direct relationship to the question of organized citizen participation.

Community Action Groups
and City Governments

Chapter One

Overview

ORGANIZED CITIZEN PARTICIPATION

The involvement of citizens in the affairs of their governments is not a new phenomenon. At the local level, the American citizen elects a substantial number of the officials who govern his community. While most citizens will not run for office or serve as an appointed member of a public commission, many may campaign for candidates of their choice, or attend a public hearing of a local governing body when their personal interests are at stake. It is still more likely that citizens will contact elected officials on occasion, and it will hardly be surprising to find them active as members of the many community groups that exist for civic purposes.

    While available studies indicate that only a small proportion of citizens engage in direct political action at the local level, these same studies suggest that a sizable number maintain an attentive interest in political issues and governmental affairs.[1] More importantly, events of recent years suggest a new emphasis on citizen participation in the policymaking processes of local government. The last decade has witnessed a broad range of attempts to institutionalize new channels for such citizen expression.[2]

    The thrust of this new movement toward institutionalization has derived from action at the federal level. Its character is typified by the kinds of recommendations for citizen involvement made by the National Advisory Commission on Civil Disorders.[3] Among other things, the Commission called for neighborhood action task forces, effective methods for processing grievances against local

1

governments, hearings by local legislative bodies on inner-city problems, establishment of neighborhood city halls as informal means
for complaints and grievances, and more effective community participation through self-determination or community control.[4]

It was in this atmosphere that the first researchers from
Urban Observatory cities (see Introduction) met to discuss methods
to be used in the citizen participation project.[5] The initial problem
was, of course, *what* citizen groups ought to be studied. After some
extended discussion, the project's work program established the
following three categories of organizations for study:

Category 1 — Citizen groups required by federal statute.
Category 2 — Locally initiated citizen groups designed to advise city
officials or governing bodies.
Category 3 — Citizen groups not recognized by ordinance or executive or legislative actions, but locally recognized by
the political process.

The first two were fairly clear-cut, but the third category needed
✓ sharper definition. In operational terms, therefore, these groups
were defined as local nonprofit voluntary organizations that attempt
to influence local governmental actions.

Since this definition implied an activist orientation, selec-
tion of groups for study was based on different kinds of issue analysis.
Researchers agreed to a pattern whereby city issues were identified
through newspaper coverage, information from local government
officials, and judgments of knowledgeable observers. Media analysis,
interviews, and questionnaires were used. Most study teams inven-
toried local citizen groups and selected key groups for more intensive
case analysis.[6]

ABOUT THE STUDY CITIES

In looking at a question as complex as organized citizen participation,
it is important to recognize that study cities differed in a number of
significant ways.[7] The cities varied in numbers of inhabitants as well
as in regional location, ranging from about 170,000 in Kansas City,
Kansas, to over 900,000 in Baltimore. They also differed in the extent to which they included the populations of their metropolitan
areas. For example, less than a fourth of Boston-area residents lived
in Boston, while the cities of Albuquerque and Nashville included
most of their metropolitan-area populations. In the majority of
cases, the central cities included about half of their metropolitan

populations. In a related way, study cities differed in terms of their population densities.

Study cities also differed considerably in types of housing stock. Those that had early growth and substantial suburban development had relatively few detached single-family houses. In Baltimore and Boston, therefore, two- to four-family and row houses were dominant, and only about 10 percent of all housing units were single-family. On the other hand, in Albuquerque and the two Kansas Cities about three-fourths or more was single-family housing, and most cities had over half of their stock in single-family units. In Milwaukee, 40 percent of the housing units were single-family structures. At the same time, Atlanta was distinctive in that over 30 percent of the housing in the city was in buildings with five or more units.

The kind of housing in a city will obviously influence the kinds of housing problems people have. In addition, this aspect of the city's physical environment may well influence the citizen's view of a whole set of urban change and development programs with which local governments are inevitably concerned. As numerous studies have established, home ownership is a major differentiating factor where citizen reactions to local government actions are concerned. Study cities varied along this dimension. In Boston, for example, less than one-third of all housing units were owner-occupied. In Albuquerque, Nashville, and the two Kansas Cities, about two-thirds of the housing units were occupied by owners.

Any assessment of the "new citizen participation" of recent years must also recognize the racial and ethnic character of the movement. The characteristics of study city populations were clearly different in this regard. Close to one-half the people in Atlanta and Baltimore were black, but less than 10 percent of those living in Albuquerque, Denver, or San Diego were black. At the same time, citizens of Spanish descent made up more than a quarter of the Albuquerque population and over 10 percent of the population in Denver. More than half the population in Boston and Milwaukee was Catholic, and about 40 percent of Albuquerque's population was also Catholic.

In traditional terms, participation in organized political or civic activity has been associated with social class—whether measured by income or education or both.[8] And, at least in its earlier stages, the new participation coming out of federally assisted urban programs involved some degree of "power to the poor."[9] On both counts, therefore, class differences in study cities should have had some bearing on both the frequency and character of organized citizen participation. While income differences—apart from regional cost-of-living factors—are likely to approximate ethnic differences, educational differences are not so apparent. And yet it may be very relevant that over 40 percent of the adult citizens in Albuquerque and San Diego had attended college, while less than one-fourth in Baltimore, Kansas City, Kansas, and Milwaukee had this experience.

Another difference among study cities—and this is far from an exhaustive list—had to do with household composition. In Atlanta and Boston, for example, almost a third of all households consisted of single individuals or unrelated roommates. In Albuquerque, Baltimore, and Nashville, such situations comprised only about a sixth of all households. As a result, Atlanta and Boston had a correspondingly lower rate of families, that is, married couples and families with children.

In sketching some of these characteristic differences among study cities, no assumption is being made that such factors explain differences in organized citizen participation. To the degree that such differences exist, the different attitudes of officials toward extra-electoral modes of participation are just as likely to be contributing. In any event, neither the project nor this book are primarily concerned with city differences in patterns of organized citizen activity. Since this book's emphasis is on common findings, differences between study cities should simply serve as a reminder that citizen participation is likely to reflect differences as well as commonalities.

INITIAL SUMMARY OF FINDINGS

Although the remaining chapters present a more organized sequence of study findings, it may be appropriate here to provide a general overview of what is to come. At the risk, therefore, of some redundancy, and without reference to particular chapters, such an overview can be sketched.

Consistent with previous research,[10] it was found that membership in city-problem-concerned groups ranged between 6 and 19 percent of the adult population. In most cities, membership averaged 13 or 14 percent. Global characteristics of study cities did not seem to affect such membership tendencies. Personal characteristics of city populations were much more explanatory. In looking at the ten-city survey population as a whole, social class, race, age level, and length of residence all had some significant relationship to membership in community groups.

Upper-class citizens were most likely to belong to organized

groups with some interest in city problems. While membership differences between whites and blacks[11] were *generally* very minor,
upper-class blacks were much more likely than upper-class whites
to have such organizational affiliations. For both groups, those older
than 34 were more likely than not to belong to city-problem-concerned groups, and this likelihood was significantly greater than for
those in the 18–34 age range. Long-term residents—those who had
lived in study cities for over 20 years—were more frequently members, and relative newcomers were much less likely to belong to such
organizations.

   With so many interrelationships and so much overlap,
cause and effect are next to impossible to determine. For example,
membership in community action groups may also be critically affected by citizens' *attitudes* toward their local governments. Using
the Urban Observatory Program's Attitude Survey data, it was possible to assess this phenomenon.

   In looking at the concept of political trust—citizen perceptions of the honesty of city officials and how well their government is being run—it was found that this had no bearing on whether
people did or did not belong to groups that were actively concerned
with problems in their cities. This is, of course, perfectly logical. If
one assumes that the citizen who is relatively trusting is likely to be
both satisfied with what his government is doing and confident of
the integrity of his local officials, then any motivation to work on
city problems would be correspondingly low. On the other hand, the
citizen with a relatively low trust level may see both government
officials and performance so negatively that he might well believe
that action on his part is not likely to change anything. In both
instances, therefore, the key to his group involvement could well
be his notion of whether his participation would make any difference.

   Another concept—political efficacy—attempts to understand the individual citizen's feelings about his personal ability to
influence the political process. Such feelings are closely related to
the idea of powerlessness, and it is usually assumed that this will
determine whether or not the individual sees it as worthwhile to
perform his civic duties or to take on civic responsibilities. In these
terms, both class and race differences were significant, with the
former being somewhat more important. Those who, in fact, lack
the influence that comes from education or income, were clearly
likely to see themselves as lacking in personal political significance.
And such perceptions did carry over into the question of membership in community groups. When citizens with average perceptions

of political efficacy were excluded from the analysis, the extremes
were related to community group membership. Citizens with a *high*
sense of political efficacy were much more likely to belong to city-
problem-concerned groups.[12]

Although the matter of such relationships is complex, such
study findings match up quite well with Hirschman's notions of exit
and voice.[13] Using this framework, one can logically assume that
people have only three basic ways of responding to problems: (1) they
can leave their neighborhoods for another area (exit); (2) they can
engage in political action (voice); or (3) they can sit silently by and
do nothing (passivity). Different social classes and races are, of course,
differently constrained in exercising such options. If one assumes
that voice is more likely to ameliorate community problems, then
both the ability and the desire of local governments to respond become critical considerations.

One of the more unique findings about community action
groups in urban areas is that, once in existence, they *will* function
when relevant issues arise. In one study city it was found that most
of the approximately two hundred groups with an expressed interest
in influencing local government did become politically active during
an observational year. In fact, many more than the original two
hundred groups were politically activated, as "extra groups" were
drawn in on the basis of neighborhood or special-interest considerations. In a very real sense, therefore, a city's community action
grouping may represent a minimum potential for organized political
action. Most community organizations—including many that may
appear to be only peripherally related to local government—can be
politicized when the occasion requires.

While cities in the citizen participation study varied in a
great many different ways, there was considerable overlap in the
kinds of issues of concern to their organized and activist citizen
groups. In most cities, housing, freeway construction, race relations,
taxation and revenue, education, and public-welfare issues were paramount. In a summary way, it can be said that most community
action groups were concerned with problems of planning and development in cities trying to provide services with an increasingly eroded
tax base. In this sense, study cities seemed to be typical of most
American cities.

Such a description may, however, be somewhat mislead-
ing. For one thing, such a crude issue summary very greatly minimizes the significance of race-relations problems. In interviews with
city officials, "community knowledgeables," and citizen-group leaders,
researchers were quick to discover that race relations permeated

much of the discussion about basic problems of the city. In those cities with significant minority populations, race relations was a fundamental theme around which a number of other issues revolved. In one city, for example, it was found that issues involving civil rights or racial conflicts were as frequently mentioned as all other issues combined. And almost twice as many citizen groups were involved with such race-related issues. These and other community issues were also politically relevant. As another city study indicated, all of the eight issues most important to community groups were major factors in that city's subsequent mayoral and councilmanic elections.

Within the context of these kinds of urban issues, researchers were particularly interested in what city officials thought about organized citizen groups, and how they preferred to deal with the community activism such groups represented. The profile of officials' beliefs about organized citizen participation was relatively easy to draw. The majority of elected representatives and appointed officials said that the concept was good—that it was important to have avenues for citizens to express their opinions and interests. At the same time, they had reservations about the ability of inner-city citizens to run their own programs; they worried about how to get democratically determined citizen leadership; and they insisted that elected officials must have final decision responsibility. Some officials—the "disbelievers"—argued that most community action groups were clique-dominated and often concerned with raising issues to justify their organizational existence.

The very familiarity of these perspectives suggests that informants were representing the modal range of city officials' attitudes. Such viewpoints also carried over into the way officials actually worked with citizen groups. Analysis of this question in study cities revealed that city officials followed a fairly predictable pattern. They usually worked closely with only one or two groups in a given community. In such instances, group leadership tended to represent an above-average income level in the community; it was generally thought to be more conservative than other segments of the community ; and the groups led were "familiar" in the sense that they had organizational ties with government or had worked before with local officials. The citizens involved usually worked closely with their councilmen. As this scenario indicates, city officials did develop expectations about how citizen groups should act. To a great degree, this involved the absence of conflict.

The citizen participation study indicated that, in one sense, citizen groups could be "successful" and "effective" through the use of many different strategies and tactics. As with most complex social phenomena, determinants of success were highly situational. In another and more pragmatic sense, however, group effectiveness may depend to a considerable degree on the ability to meet expectations of local government officials. The studies under discussion suggest that "successful" community action groups are cooperative rather than conflict-oriented. They are groups that have assembled some economic and political resources, and have some prior negotiating success. Such successful groups used their problem-related information in simple and forthright ways, and they made the kind of demands that could be politically acceded to.

It appears that most city officials are still rather conservative about newer forms of organized citizen participation. If, therefore, a citizen group is to be effective, it will probably require a small dedicated leadership cadre within its larger, more general membership structure. If local government or some part of it is to be the group's target, then this leadership group will need to understand the structure and operations of the target—to learn how "the system" works. While many community-action groups in cities seem to have learned these and related lessons, there is little evidence that most city officials have gone very far toward understanding what their communities' citizen groups are really all about.

ORGANIZATION OF THIS BOOK

Chapter 2 presents an analysis of relevant data from the Urban Observatory Program's Citizens' Attitude Survey.[14] The focus is on community action groups in study cities—initially defined as clubs, neighborhood groups, or other organizations working on city problems in some way. This assessment involves both the individual city as the unit of analysis, and citizen survey samples from ten cities treated as a single combined sample. The emphasis is on the latter, with organizational membership examined from the vantage point of a set of personal and attitudinal variables.

Chapter 3 deals with problems of classifying community groups. Although a number of classification approaches used in individual study cities are illustrated, the emphasis is on the development of a conceptual scheme for classifying community-action groups. Chapter 4 draws from the issue-analysis work done in most study cities. Basic issues associated with community-action groups are identified, classified, interpreted, and otherwise commented on. Chapter 5 confronts the thorny question of appraising the effectiveness of community action groups. As in other assessments of this question, findings are based on an analysis of perceptions—with some support from observational analysis. Chapter 6 sums up; establishes some frames of reference for appraising study outcomes; considers some of the implications of study findings; and speculates about future citizen participation in the study's areas of concern.

Appendix A provides a number of survey data summary tables—information relating to the Chapter 2 discussion of material from the Citizens' Attitude Survey. Appendix B refers the reader to the basic city studies underlying this synthesis. As noted earlier, Appendix B also samples the individual city studies. Appendix C provides some basic references to recent and still current bibliographies in areas connected with the subject matters of the Urban Observatory Program's citizen participation study.[15]

NOTES

1. See, for example, the summaries on power, politics, and participation in John C. Bollens and Henry J. Schmandt, *The Metropolis: Its People, Politics, and Economic Life* (2nd ed.; New York: Harper & Row, 1970), pp. 126–161.
2. The literature on this "new citizen participation" is now extraordinarily voluminous. Although there is no single best source, most of the subject matters usually associated with the term are covered in special issues (September 1972 and October 1972) or symposia (January/February 1969 and May/June 1972) of the *Public Administration Review*. For summarizing reviews of this new citizen participation movement, see in particular Carl W. Stenberg, "Citizens and the Administrative State: From Participation to Power," *Public Administration Review* 32 (May/June 1972): 190–198; and Henry J. Schmandt, "Municipal Decentralization: An Overview," *Public Administration Review* 32 (October 1972): 571–588.
3. See *Report of the National Advisory Commission on Civil Disorders* (New York: Bantam Books, 1968).
4. For a new standard reference, see Alan Altshuler, *Community Control: The Black Demand for Participation in Large American Cities* (New York: Pegasus, 1970).
5. In the interest of objectivity, it should be noted that studying citizen participation groups was selected as the Urban Observatory Program's first cooperative network project (by the initial six Observatory cities) because the matter was of significant concern to two or three cities. Most other cities had no strong objections, and the four cities subsequently entering the program participated as a condition of membership.
6. These definitions and understandings comprised the general framework for the project's cooperative efforts.

7. Most of these descriptions of study cities is drawn from the special report publication on the Citizens' Attitude Survey. See note 6 to the Introduction, above.

8. A now definitive reference is Sidney Verba and Norman H. Nie, *Participation in America: Political Democracy and Social Equality* (New York: Harper & Row, 1972).

9. This is *not* to say that the origins of the "new participation" were primarily economic. They were, of course, significantly influenced by the total civil rights movement of the 1960s. See Charles V. Hamilton, "Blacks and the Crisis in Political Participation," *The Public Interest* 34 (Winter 1972): 188–210.

10. See, for example, Amos H. Hawley and Basil G. Zimmer, *The Metropolitan Community: Its People and Government* (Beverly Hills: Sage Publications, 1970), pp. 55–58.

11. For purposes of this book's analysis of data from the Citizens' Attitude Survey project, the terms white and whites *exclude* whites of Spanish descent, and the terms black and blacks *include* a small number of other non-white respondents. Where the term minority population is used, it includes blacks as just defined *or* Spanish descent whites (as the primary minority group in three study cities). Primary comparisons are, therefore, between non-Spanish descent whites (some 70% of the combined ten-city survey sample) and blacks (approximatey 21% of the combined sample) and a small number of other non-white respondents (some 2% of the combined sample).

12. There is, again, an enormous and varied literature that deals in one way or another with the concepts of political trust and political efficacy. The general frame of reference for this book's analysis derives from David Easton, *A Systems Analysis of Political Life* (New York: Wiley, 1965); William Gamson, *Power and Discontent* (Homewood, Illinois: Dorsey, 1968); Joel D. Aberbach and Jack L. Walker, "Political Trust and Racial Ideology," *American Political Science Review* 64 (December 1970): 1199–1219; and Ada Finifter, "Dimensions of Political Alienation," *American Political Science Review* 64 (June 1970): 389–410.

13. For a full discussion of these concepts, see Albert O. Hirschman, *Exit, Voice and Loyalty: Responses to Decline in Firms, Organizations and States* (Cambridge, Mass.: Harvard University Press, 1970).

14. These particular data were not intended for use in the Urban Observatory Program's Citizens' Attitude Survey project. They were supplied by the Project Director for use in the citizen participation project. These data are identified in Chapter 2 and Appendix A as Recoded data.

15. Beyond normal literature searches for relevant background studies and data, the focus of the study of organized citizen participation was on new and original research within a specific network of cooperating cities. As Appendix C indicates, the Kansas City, Kansas and Atlanta studies involved significant literature reviews.

Chapter Two

Membership in Community
Groups

ORGANIZATIONAL MEMBERSHIP IN STUDY
CITIES

An earlier Urban Observatory Program report summarized findings
of responses to 4300 in-depth interviews in ten observatory cities.[1]
The adults surveyed represented a cross-section of each city's
population and their responses included views and feelings about
city government, city services, and city problems. They were asked
many specific questions, and a few of their responses related to
issues connected with organized citizen participation. The survey
was carried out in ten of the cities (all but Cleveland) in the citizen
participation study. It is useful, therefore, to begin discussion of
organized citizen participation in study cities by drawing from this
survey's data.[2]

In seeking background information from those interviewed,
survey people asked, "Do you belong to any clubs, neighborhood
groups, or other organizations that are working on city problems in
any way?" Proportions claiming such memberships ranged from 6.2
percent in Kansas City, Kansas, to 19.1 percent in Atlanta.[3]
While some might see these proportions as small, they were generally
consistent with findings from other investigations. For example,
people in urban areas are far less likely to participate in formal
organizations than they are to engage in informal associations. The
majority have no organizational memberships apart from union or
church ties, and no more than a fifth are likely to belong to
organizations that are more or less directly concerned with community
welfare. In central cities, membership in such community and civic
groups will average 13 or 14 percent.[4]

On an overall basis, therefore, study cities appeared to

be typical. At the same time, there were real differences between some study cities as far as memberships in city-problem-concerned organizations were concerned. In these terms, Atlanta and Baltimore were quite different from Kansas City, Kansas and Milwaukee, while the other six cities did not significantly differ from each other or any of the remaining four.[5]

Although it is generally assumed that the number of "joiners" increases as the size of place declines, analysis indicated no clear relationship between adult populations and membership in the kinds of organizations covered by the survey. The smallest city (Kansas City, Kansas) had the smallest proportion, while the next smallest (Albuquerque) was relatively high up on the membership scale. Baltimore (the largest city) was next to the top in membership proportions, while Atlanta (the city with the top membership rank) was relatively far down on the adult population scale.[6]

The survey question used was quite general. It covered many different kinds of groups, and it allowed for personal interpretation of what it meant for an organization to be "working on city problems." Most of the groups named were, however, classifiable as either: (1) civic bodies, fraternal groups, educational or youth-serving organizations, and church groups; or (2) neighborhood associations, political clubs, and civil rights organizations. Most members were involved with the former kinds of groups, with only a fourth or so belonging to neighborhood organizations.

It seemed possible, therefore, that membership on a neighborhood basis might have had some relationship to such characteristics as population densities and minority-group population proportions. As with the other analysis, however, there was no clear and consistent relationship. Baltimore, the most populated city—comparatively dense and with a very large black population—had the largest proportion belonging to neighborhood groups. On the other hand, Boston—somewhat smaller but denser and with a much smaller minority population proportion—also had a relatively large proportion of neighborhood-group members.[7] The pattern in the remaining eight cities continued to be erratic. This indicates that a complex of other factors was affecting membership in both neighborhood and other city-problem-concerned groups.[8]

Chapter 1 noted that political participation has been traditionally associated with social class. The more educated citizenry has tended to be more politically active.[9] At the same time, those with higher incomes or higher occupational status may or may not be more organizationally involved with political, civic, or community affairs. In looking at this question in study cities (taken as a whole), a social-class index was constructed to group those interviewed as upper, middle, or lower class. The index combined educational attainment and total family income factors. The relationships of social class, so measured, to membership in city-problem-concerned groups, is outlined in Table 2-1.

Table 2-1. Organizational Membership and Social Class

Membership Classification	Upper Class	Middle Class	Lower Class
Members	35.04%	51.58%	13.38%
Nonmembers	16.04	59.46	24.50
Total Survey Group	19.20%	60.70%	20.10%

Source: Recoded data, Urban Observatory Program's Citizens' Attitude Survey, 1972.

As statistical analysis demonstrates, social class was a significantly discriminating variable.[10] Upper-class citizens—in this instance, people with education at or beyond the high school graduation level, with annual family incomes approaching or exceeding $15,000—were more likely to belong to organizations with some interest in city problems. Middle- and lower-class segments of the citizenry—those with less formal education/or family income— were much less likely to belong to such groups.

For the most part, these class differences held up across racial lines. In a general sense, race did not make any group-membership difference, but in a more specific sense, it did. In comparing whites in study cities (excluding those of Spanish descent) with blacks, it was found that racial differences were quite insignificant.[11] Thus social class continued to make a significant difference when race was controlled. As Table 2-2 illustrates, however, a significant racial difference did exist at the upper-class level.

Table 2-2. Social Class, Race, and Organizational Membership

Social Class by Race	% Survey Group	% Membership	% Nonmembership
White[a] Upper Class	16.7	24.56	75.44
Black[b] Upper Class	2.5	40.69	59.31
White Middle Class	43.9	12.64	87.63
Black Middle Class	14.4	13.42	86.58
White Lower Class	15.1	8.54	91.46
Black Lower Class	7.4	9.02	90.98
Total Survey Group		14.15%	85.85%

[a]Excludes people of Spanish descent.
[b]Includes small numbers of other non-white groups.
Source: Recoded data, Urban Observatory Program's Citizens' Attitude Survey, 1972.

Upper-class citizens—both whites and blacks—were clearly more likely to be organizationally involved with city problems than middle- and lower-class people, white or black. At the same time, middle-and lower-class blacks were just as likely as whites of the same classes to belong to groups concerned with city problems. But upper-class blacks were much more likely to have such affiliations.

Although there appear to be no immediate reasons why this difference existed, it should be noted that the difference persisted when levels of expressed interest in city problems were examined. Another survey question asked representative people in study cities, "How interested would you say you are in city problems and city politics—*very interested, fairly interested,* or *not too interested?*" As with the organizational-membership question, social class turned out to be a significant factor, with upper-class citizens more frequently claiming a greater interest level.

This time, however, race also made a significant difference. As Table 2- 3 demonstrates, blacks consistently asserted proportionately greater interest in city problems and politics. In the "fairly interested" category, both race and class differences flatten out and neither is very significant. Blacks are, however, more frequently "very interested" and much less likely to reflect very limited degrees of interest. These differences are apparent at all class levels. When one looks at the "not too interested" category, however, the greatest racial disparity is at the upper-class level.

The available literature on the community membership tendencies of Americans also suggests that such "joining behavior" is a function of both age and length of residence. Here again, study cities fit into this established pattern. Table 2- 4 shows those interviewed grouped into three general age classifications. As Table 2- 4 indicates, the age grouping to which a citizen belonged was significant. Those older than 34 were more likely than not to belong to city-problem-concerned groups, and the likelihood was significantly greater than among those in the 18- 34 age range.

Table 2- 5 demonstrates that length of city residence was also a factor contributing to membership. Long-term residents—defined here as those who had lived in the city for at least 21 years—were more frequently involved with city-problem-concerned groups, and those who were relative newcomers were much less likely to belong to such organizations.

There is obviously much in the way of overlap as far as these factors are concerned. While some study cities were organizationally different, most were not too dissimilar. Where city differences did exist, such gross factors as population size, density,

Table 2-3. Race, Social Class, and Interest in City Affairs

Race by Social Class	% of Survey Group	Very Interested	Fairly Interested	Not too Interested
White[a] Upper Class	16.7%	32.7%	50.0%	17.3%
Black[b] Upper Class	2.5	45.3	53.5	1.2
White Middle Class	43.9	23.4	53.8	22.8
Black Middle Class	14.4	44.3	46.5	9.2
White Lower Class	15.1	18.7	45.6	35.8
Black Lower Class	7.4	35.5	43.3	21.2

[a]Excludes people of Spanish descent.
[b]Includes small numbers of other non-white groups.
Source: Recoded Data, Urban Observatory Program's Citizens' Attitude Survey, 1972.

Table 2-4. Organizational Membership and Age Groupings (% by age groups)

Membership Classification	Ages 18-34	Ages 35-64	Ages 65 & over
Members	29.13%	55.99%	14.88%
Nonmembers	38.80	47.51	13.69
Total Survey Group	37.40%	48.80%	13.80%

Source: Recoded data, Urban Observatory Program's Citizens' Attitude Survey, 1972.

Table 2-5. Organizational Membership and Length of Residence (% by residence)

Membership Classification	Newcomers (5 years or less)	Intermediates (6 to 20 years)	Oldtimers (21 years or more)
Members	13.91%	28.63%	57.46%
Nonmembers	20.12	27.79	52.09
Total Survey Group	19.3%	27.9%	52.8%

Source: Recoded data, Urban Observatory Program's Citizens' Attitude Survey, 1972.

and size of minority-group population were not explanatory. Looking across the study cities, however, social class, certain aspects of race, age range, and length of residence all had some significant bearing on these particular kinds of organizational involvements. These *same* factors similarly related to stated levels of interest in city problems and city politics. It is logical to expect, therefore, that they may also have related to more *specific* attitudes about city government performance. If so, such attitudes would help to explain more about who belongs to the kinds of groups that are potentially involved with city governments.

POLITICAL TRUST AND GROUP MEMBERSHIP

The concept of political trust is defined in various ways. Usually, however, it refers to citizen perceptions of how well government officials are living up to public expectations. In operational terms, this involves questions of how honest officials are and how well government is being run. Such perceptions could, of course, have a potential influence on organized citizen participation. If one assumes that citizen groups can and will generate requests or demands for certain kinds of actions by city government, then both the frequency and character of such demands may be affected by the level of trust in government.

The following six items in the Urban Observatory Program's Citizens' Attitude Survey dealt with political trust questions.[12]

1. On the whole, do you think local government officials are more honest on their jobs than most other people, say people in business, are about the same, or are they less honest than most other people?
2. In some cities, officials are said to take bribes and make money in other ways that are illegal. In other cities such things almost never happen. How much of that sort of thing do you think goes on in [interviewee's city]?
3. Over the past 5 or 10 years, do you think that local government here in [interviewee's city] has gotten better, has stayed about the same, or do you think it is not as good as it used to be?
4. And overall, how would you rate the way [interviewee's city] is run?
5. Considering what people in [interviewee's city] pay in local taxes, do you think the people generally get their money's worth in services or not?
6. Thinking of all public services—fire and police protection, schools, parks, transportation (trash collection), street maintenance, and other things—do you think the services here in this neighborhood are generally better than in other parts of [interviewee's city], are they about the same, or are they not as good as in other parts of the city?

For purposes of this citizen participation analysis, a political trust index for each citizen interviewed was constructed. Weights were assigned for alternative responses, and scores for all six items were summed to obtain an individual political trust score.

This trust index produced scores ranging from 6 to 26, with a higher score reflecting a greater degree of confidence in city government. Individual scores were averaged to determine mean scores for study cities.[13]

There were no clear and consistent relationships between city trust scores and the frequency of membership in groups concerned with city problems. As with the relationship between organizational membership and the size of a city's population, the relationship between membership and average trust level was random. The same was generally true of trust scores and membership in neighborhood groups. Baltimore and Boston were the cities with the largest proportions of citizens belonging to neighborhood groups, and they also ranked at the bottom on the political trust index. At the same time, however, the two Kansas Cities were near the bottom of the index and, in those cities, the frequency of citizens in neighborhood groups was less than in all of the other cities.[14] There were, however, some relationships that were more clear-cut. These are summarized in Table 2-6.

Table 2-6. Neighborhood Groups, Average Trust Scores, Population Densities, and Minority-Group Proportions

City	Neighborhood Group Membership Rank	Mean Political Trust Score Rank	Population Density Rank	Minority-Group Proportion Rank
Baltimore	1	9	2	2
Boston	2	10	1	6
Denver	3	4	5	8
Atlanta	4	5	8	1
San Diego	5	1	9	9
Albuquerque	6	2	6	10
Nashville	7	6	10	4.5
Milwaukee	8	3	4	7
Kansas City, Missouri	9	8	7	3
Kansas City, Kansas	10	7	3	4.5

Source: Recoded data, Urban Observatory Program's Citizens' Attitude Survey, 1972.

As noted, there was no very strong relationship observed between membership in city-problem-concerned neighborhood groups and a city's average trust score. The same was true of the relationships between such membership and a city's population density and the proportion of its minority (blacks or Spanish descent whites) population.

The most significant relationships were between average trust scores and density and minority population ranks. There was a fairly large *negative* relationship (R of -0.54) between relative mean score on the political trust index and population density. This suggests a tendency toward lower levels of confidence in local government in cities that were (comparatively) more densely populated. There was an even larger *negative* relationship (R of -0.66) between the average level of trust and the proportion of minority-group citizens in the city's population. This suggests the not very surprising tendency for cities with significant black or Spanish descent populations to evidence somewhat lower overall levels of political trust.

It should be stressed, however, that these two general tendencies reflected *separate* phenomena, which may or may not be related in a given situation. On an overall ten-city basis, there was no consistent relationship (R of 0.05) between density and minority-group population factors. On a different kind of an overall basis—taking all those interviewed in all study cities as a single group— it was clear that social class and racial characteristics were most significantly related to a citizen's level of political trust.

As with membership in city-problem-concerned groups, social class was significantly related to degree of political trust (see Table 2-7). Social class, as defined in this analysis, was clearly discriminating. Upper-class citizens—those with average or better educations and annual family incomes at or beyond $15,000—were

Table 2-7. Social Class and Levels of Political Trust

Social Classes in Survey Group	Trust Scores of 6 through 13	Trust Scores of 14 through 17	Trust Scores of 18 through 26
Upper Class	20.6%	32.0%	47.4%
Middle Class	28.6	38.1	33.3
Lower Class	29.5	37.5	33.0
Total Survey Group	27.3%	37.0%	35.7%

Source: Recoded data, Urban Observatory Program's Citizens' Attitude Survey, 1972.

much more likely than their less-advantaged fellow citizens to exhibit higher levels of trust in their local governments.

Unlike the organizational membership situation, however, race was about equally influential in affecting political trust levels (see Table 2-8). The data here are rather unequivocal. Whites were significantly more likely than blacks to have comparatively high levels of trust, and significantly less likely to have comparatively low levels. With both races, however, there was a "middle third" that evidenced somewhat mixed perspectives.

Table 2-8. Race and Levels of Political Trust

Races in Survey Group	Trust Scores of 6 through 13	Trust Scores of 14 through 17	Trust Scores of 18 through 26
White[a]	24.2%	36.7%	39.1%
Black[b]	34.3	37.4	28.3
Total Survey Group	27.3%	37.0%	35.7%

[a]Excludes people of Spanish descent.
[b]Includes small numbers of other non-white groups.
Source: Recoded data, Urban Observatory Program's Citizens' Attitude Survey, 1972.

Since the measure of trust used involved a mix of perceptions of political integrity (the two "honesty of officials" questions) *and* governmental competence (the remaining "government performance" and "management" questions), social class and race factors were not mutually exclusive. This is demonstrated in Table 2-9. Inspection of this table indicates that *both* class and race factors were simultaneously influencing political trust attitudes. On

Table 2-9. Social Class, Race, and Levels of Political Trust

Social Classes by Race in Survey Group	Trust Scores of 6 through 13	Trust Scores of 14 through 17	Trust Scores of 18 through 26
White[a] Upper Class	18.6%	32.0%	49.4%
Black[b] Upper Class	30.0	33.7	30.3
White Middle Class	25.8	38.6	35.6
Black Middle Class	40.1	36.8	23.1
White Lower Class	27.9	36.5	35.6
Black Lower Class	33.6	41.0	25.4
Total Survey Group	27.3%	37.0%	35.7%

[a]Excludes people of Spanish descent.
[b]Includes small numbers of other non-white groups.
Source: Recoded data, Urban Observatory Program's Citizens' Attitude Survey, 1972.

a class basis, there was a general tendency for white and black upper-class people to have more higher trust scores and fewer lower trust scores than middle- and lower-class citizens. The direction was not, however, completely consistent, since the black middle class was more likely than the black lower class to have more negative views. In virtually every instance, however, whites manifested higher levels of trust than their black class equivalents. Such racial differences were concentrated at both the above-average and below-average levels of political trust. At the intermediate level (scores 14 through 17), neither class nor race differences were very large.

With this degree of complexity involved, there is no reason to expect that trust levels would relate in any particular way to membership in groups concerned with city problems. Social class did so relate, as it did to levels of political trust. Race (except at the upper-class level) did *not* relate to membership, and it did to trust levels. These variables apparently exerted certain cancelling out effects that resulted in no clear relationship between organizational membership and trust level.[15] Although larger proportions of organizational members had higher trust scores, and smaller proportions demonstrated lower scores, differences were not statistically significant. No matter how the various scores are rearranged, the level of the citizen's trust in his local government had no significant bearing on whether he was or was not a member of a city-problem-concerned group.

Apart from the fact that some of the survey's groups may have had only indirect involvements with local government, there is no logical reason why political trust and such group membership *ought* to be related. As the summary of findings in Chapter 1 noted, the citizen who is very trusting is likely to be satisfied with what his government is doing and confident of the integrity of his local officials. His motivation to work on city problems would be correspondingly low. On the other hand, citizens with relatively low trust levels might see government officials and performance so negatively that they believe their involvement would not change anything. In both instances, therefore, the key to involvement could be the notion of whether participation would make any kind of a meaningful difference.

POLITICAL EFFICACY AND GROUP MEMBERSHIP

The concept of political efficacy deals with the citizen's feelings about his personal ability to influence the political process. Such feelings are closely related to the idea of powerlessness. It is usually assumed that this will determine whether or not an individual sees it as worthwhile to perform his civic duties or to take on civic responsibilities. The following three items in the Urban Observatory Program's attitude survey touched upon such considerations.

1. Which officials or other people do you think really run the local government here in [interviewee's city]—which people make the most difference in how well the city is run?
2. How much do you think the people who count in local government here in [interviewee's city] are concerned about the same problems you are concerned about?
3. What do you think is the best way people like you can make themselves heard by city government?

Coding and weighting alternatives and summing item scores produced a usable political efficacy index. Scores ranged from 3 to 15, with a higher score indicating a greater belief that personal action as a ' citizen makes sense. As with the political trust index, mean city scores were computed. Study cities evidenced few differences in terms of such scores.[16]

Unlike political-trust rankings, however, a city's mean efficacy score *was* somewhat related to organizational membership— ' the relative proportion of adults belonging to groups concerned with city problems.

Table 2-10 indicates there was an *inverse* relationship (R of —0.59). Kansas City, Kansas and Milwaukee, the two cities .

Table 2-10. Organizational Memberships and Average Efficacy Scores

City	Organizational Membership Rank	Mean Political Efficacy Score Rank	Neighborhood Group Membership Rank
Atlanta	1	10	4
Baltimore	2	5	1
Denver	3	6	3
Albuquerque	4	9	6
Nashville	5	3	7
San Diego	6	4	5
Boston	7	7	2
Kansas City, Missouri	8	8	9
Milwaukee	9	2	8
Kansas City, Kansas	10	1	10

Sources: Original data and recoded data, Urban Observatory Program's Citizens' Attitude Survey, 1971 and 1972.

with the highest mean efficacy scores, were also the cities with the smallest proportions of organizational memberships. At the same time, Atlanta, the city with the lowest average score, had the largest proportion of people as members of city-problem-concerned groups. Since very few organizations covered by the survey were *expressly* designed for political purposes, it is not at all clear what meaning should be attached to this relationship.[17]

There was also a relationship between a citizen's sense of political efficacy and the tendency to belong to city-problem-concerned kinds of organizations. On an overall basis, however, this relationship was not significant.[18] Although nonmember respondents tended to have more efficacy scores at the lower end of the distribution, this difference was not statistically significant.

If, however, citizens who scored at or near the *average* level (using an overall mean of 8.2) are eliminated from consideration, the picture changes. Relationships depicted in Table 2-11 are significant. They indicate that citizens with political efficacy scores above the average were more likely to belong to city-problem-concerned groups.

Table 2-11. Organizational Membership and Levels of Political Efficacy

Membership Classification	Efficacy Scores of 3 through 7	Efficacy Scores of 9 through 15
Members	32.5%	67.5%
Nonmembers	41.1	58.9
Total Survey Group	40.0%	60.0%

Source: Recoded data, Urban Observatory Program's Citizens' Attitude Survey, 1972.

There were, of course, other factors at work. As with political trust, the political efficacy index used was significantly related to both social class and race. These relationships were in the anticipated direction. Upper-class citizens were more likely to see their political efforts as potentially effective, and whites, more than blacks, were likely to reflect this same pattern. Table 2-12 outlines the detailed character of these differences.

The class pattern is consistent for blacks—in the sense that upper-class people manifested fewer low efficacy scores and many more high scores than did the middle and lower classes. Middle- and lower-class blacks were similarly differentiated. The class pattern for whites, however, was more erratic. The distance between low

Table 2-12. Social Class, Race, and Levels of Political Efficacy—I

Social Classes By Race in Survey Group	*Efficacy Scores 3 through 7*	*Efficacy Scores 8 through 9*	*Efficacy Scores 10 through 15*
White[a] Upper Class	23.5%	52.4%	24.1%
Black[b] Upper Class	24.4	44.4	31.2
White Middle Class	29.7	30.5	39.8
Black Middle Class	33.2	39.8	27.0
White Lower Class	40.2	41.3	18.5
Black Lower Class	45.7	37.5	16.8
Total Survey Group	31.8%	43.8%	24.4%

[a]Excludes people of Spanish descent.
[b]Includes small numbers of other non-white groups.
Source: Recoded data, Urban Observatory Program's Citizens' Attitude Survey, 1972.

efficacy scores for white upper- and middle-class groupings was modest, and white middle-class people had a much larger number of high scores than either lower- *or* upper-class whites.

It would be incorrect, however, to interpret this as middle-class whites believing very strongly in the effectiveness of their personal political behavior. When near-average scores were removed, class patterns became more typical. As Table 2-13 indicates, with this correction, class differences become completely consistent.

Table 2-13. Social Class, Race, and Levels of Political Efficacy—II

Social Classes by Race in Survey Group	*Efficacy Scores of 3 through 7*	*Efficacy Scores of 9 through 15*
White[a] Upper Class	30.0%	70.0%
Black[b] Upper Class	32.3	67.7
White Middle Class	36.5	63.5
Black Middle Class	42.1	57.9
White Lower Class	49.8	50.2
Black Lower Class	55.7	44.3
Total Survey Group	39.6%	60.4%

[a]Excludes people of Spanish descent.
[b]Includes small numbers of other non-white groups.
Source: Recoded data, Urban Observatory Program's Citizens' Attitude Survey, 1972.

On either basis (Table 2-12 or 2-13), race differences for low efficacy scores were in the expected direction. Fewer whites than blacks evidenced such low scores. With high efficacy scores, the picture was mixed. When all scores were considered (Table 2-12), both upper- and middle-class blacks tended to have greater efficacy feelings than upper-class whites. This was again, however, a function of a black upper- and middle-class clustering of beliefs around the average efficacy level. When this factor is eliminated, race differences for high efficacy scores are as anticipated.

At the same time, racial distances were not as great—particularly at the extremes and at the upper-class level—as they were on the social-class dimension. Differences between the white middle and lower classes—again at the low and high ends of the index—were very similar to those of blacks at the same levels. It would appear, therefore, that class was somewhat more important in explaining citizens' perceptions of their political relevance.

As is usually the case in complex social systems, everything tended to relate to everything else. Political trust and efficacy attitudes related to social class and to race, as well as to levels of expressed interest in city problems and city politics. Political efficacy levels, in low- and high-score terms, significantly related to membership in city-problem-concerned groups. When political trust and political efficacy levels are considered together—and such combinations are then analyzed across race-class categories—the configuration becomes quite complicated.[19]

CONCLUSIONS

As analysis of survey data has demonstrated, understanding who participates in citizen groups concerned with city problems is a complex matter. The global characteristics of study cities provide little in the way of insight. Personal characteristics of city populations are much more explanatory. Taking the study cities as a whole, it is evident that social class and race were major variables. Both related to membership in city-problem-concerned organizations—as did age level and length of city residence. They also related to expressed levels of interest in local affairs, with blacks of all social classes more frequently claiming higher levels of interest.

Political attitudes—including political trust and, to an even greater degree, political efficacy—related to class and race variables, and both directly and indirectly to group membership. Taken as a whole, therefore, survey information has many utilities in helping to explain some of the general "characteristics" of organizational participation.

NOTES

1. See note 6 of the Introduction, above.
2. It should be noted here that the Project Director for the Citizens' Attitude Survey bears no responsibility for analysis or other treatment of survey data used in this citizen participation project report.
3. See Table A-1.
4. See, for example, note 10 to Chapter 1, above.
5. See Table A-2.
6. Ibid.
7. The Baltimore and Boston patterns would probably become *consistent* (rather than disparate) if the well-known "white ethnicity" of Boston's neighborhoods were taken into account—if "minority population" were redefined to include both blacks and white ethnics.
8. See Table A-3.
9. Verba and Nie sum up this widely accepted generalization in finding upper-middle-class white males dominant among activists in political affairs, with clear overrepresentation compared to the general population. Conversely, those with lower social status—blacks, the young, and to some degree women—are more likely to be politically passive. See page 97 of the Verba-Nie citation (n.8) to Chapter 1, above.
10. Analysis of survey data involved the use of the Chi-square method. In all instances and with regard to all references in this book, significance was at, and most frequently well beyond, the 0.05 level of confidence.
11. See Table A-4.
12. Since the survey instrument developed for the Citizens' Attitude Survey did not employ standardized trust and efficacy items, it was necessary to use those available items that could be analytically grouped to create political trust and political efficacy indexes.
13. See Table A-5.
14. See Table A-6.
15. See Table A-7.
16. See Table A-8.
17. All kinds of speculations are, of course, possible. For example, these data might suggest that greater efficacy feelings are associated with some greater general satisfaction with established political structures or processes, or, conversely, that concerned groups are more likely to come into being when needs for supplementary modes of contact and influence are perceived.
18. See Table A-9.
19. See Table A-10.

Chapter Three

Classifying Community Action Groups

SURVEY GROUPS AND PROJECT GROUPS

The city-problem-concerned groups covered by the Urban Observatory Program's attitude survey make up what some have called the parapolitical structure of the community. These are the kinds of groups that permit people of like interests to combine and pool their resources for a wide variety of purposes. While most are not specifically oriented to politics or city affairs, many can become "politicized"—that is, many seek to further their aims through governmental action. As Bollens and Schmandt note, "it is no exaggeration to say that these organizations are a precondition for the translation of individual desires into social action."[1]

Virtually all survey groups could be categorized as: political/ civil rights; educational/youth serving; civic/fraternal; church; health/ social welfare; ad hoc neighborhood; or government affiliated neighborhood. In this sense, therefore, they clearly "fit" as elements in the parapolitical structures of citizen participation study cities. As noted, however, not all such organizations are *primarily* interested in or have any *substantial* concern with local public affairs.

Community action groups—those that are primarily concerned with local issues—involve a smaller proportion of the population, but it was primarily this more restricted set of citizen organizations that Urban Observatory project study teams investigated.[2] The overall study design embraced government-connected organizations— required by federal law or initiated by local government—and local citizen groups seeking to influence government action. For purposes of this analysis, these broad categories will be referred to hereafter as *federal, city* and *voluntary* groups. The project's study approach assumed, therefore, that this classification method would cover just about all community action organizations. Since local groups were to be identified through their connection with local issues, this approach would likely encompass any local citizen group that was visibly change-oriented. It would be fair to say, therefore, that study cities were *generally* interested in better defining their then-current parapolitical situations, while they were *particularly* interested in understanding the newer and more aggressive groups on their community action scenes.[3]

APPROACHES TO CLASSIFICATION

Most study city researchers engaged in some degree of classification work. At the same time, however, three somewhat different emphases seemed to be involved. Some were primarily interested in "assembling the picture"—that is, in identifying groups around community issues or in constructing a full working inventory of the community's organized citizen groups. Others attempted to put together an analytical scheme that would permit more detailed description and more adequate comparison of such groups. Still others were concerned with distinguishing "active" from "passive" groups—those that might have related to government, but did not—and those that *did* so relate during the study period. In a majority of cases, researchers were involved with a mix of such classification activities.

The Atlanta study[4] illustrates the first situation: an attempt to identify groups around community issues. In a year's sampling of metropolitan and local newspapers, researchers were able to locate 92 different citizen groups that had taken a stand or been active around a local public issue. The working arrangement of these groups is depicted in Table 3-1. As the table indicates, this city's broad range of issue-concerned citizen bodies could be generally grouped into 23 somewhat specific categories. These categories could, in turn, be collapsed into 6 still broader categories on the basis of sponsorship, member composition, organizational purpose, political concern, or geographic factors. All fell within the project's criteria, in the sense that they were either federal or city groups, or voluntary groups of a local nonprofit kind that were attempting to influence local government action.

The Atlanta study's very general categories were somewhat overlapping, and its initial classification scheme in no sense represented an adequate design for comparative analysis of organized

Table 3-1. Issue-Concerned Citizen Groups: Classification in a Study City

Category[a]	Subcategory[b]	Numbers in Categories & Subcategories	Percent of Total[c]
Public Programs		17	18%
	Federal Programs	5	5%
	City Programs	3	3
	Government Planning	9	10
Occupational		21	23
	Professional	12	13
	Union	2	2
	Business-Special Interest	3	3
	Business-Fraternal	2	2
	Business-Young Businessmen	2	2
Social Welfare		13	14
	Traditional Service	4	5
	Traditional Planning	3	3
	Church Sponsored	3	3
	Community Action	3	3
Rights-Protest		27	30
	Civil Rights (National Group)	5	5
	Civil Rights (Local Coalition)	2	2
	Other Rights (National Group)	3	3
	Student-Youth Protest (National Group)	3	3
	Student-Youth Protest (Local Group)	4	5
	Peace (Local Group)	3	3
	Education (Local Group)	4	5
	Church (Local Group)	3	3
Political Action		6	6
	Political Party (Local Affiliates)	2	2
	Organized Voters (Local Groups)	4	5
Neighborhood		8	9
	Civic Associations—Clubs	8	9

[a]Within each category, subcategories are ordered by general degree of formal organization, from greater to lesser.

[b]Terms are short forms of narrative descriptions.

[c]Percentages rounded throughout table.

Source: Adapted from *General Survey of Organized Citizen Participation* (Atlanta Urban Observatory, 1970).

citizen groups. As will be noted, both here and in other study cities, groups were concerned with quite different kinds of public and community issues. At the same time, the Atlanta study's broad categories for issue-concerned groups matched up quite well with the survey project's grouping of city-problem-concerned organizations. This demonstrated again that *all* such citizen groups were *potentially* involved in community affairs in ways that were somehow politically relevant. As noted above, *all* parapolitical groups may become "politicized" in trying to further their organizational objectives.[5]

In contrast to Atlanta's somewhat informal functional approach, the study in Kansas City, Missouri had the creation of a classified inventory as its primary research objective. This study's methods involved detailed examination of some 150 of almost 1000 of the estimated 1200 citizen groups in that city. Using the project's three basic categories of citizen groups as a starting point, 21 subcategories were identified.

With this inventory approach, researchers developed a directory that defined basic organizational and membership characteristics for each subcategory. All the subcategories in Table 3-2 could be rearranged to fit the other general classification formats that have been noted.

In generalizing about the citizen participation project's three-level classification approach as it applied to Kansas City, Missouri, researchers there noted the following:

1. The availability of federal funds constituted the basis for and the dynamics of federal groups initiated during the sixties.
2. As organizations seeking to create cooperation for community development purposes, such federal groups were hindered by the unfavorable characteristics of their target areas.
3. City groups initiated before the sixties to fill a political communications gap tended to have more racial balance and organizational stability, and tended to manifest more conservative and less tension-producing attitudes, than those federal groups established in the sixties.
4. At the same time, the scale of issues, projects and funds was smaller than with federal urban programs, and the majority of these city groups would probably have disappeared if city hall had withdrawn its organizing and financial support.
5. Voluntary groups were highly differentiated in that this category simultaneously included both the least and the most politically conscious groups—as well as the most conservative and the most radical organizations.

Table 3-2. Government and Voluntary Citizen Groups: Classification
in a Study City

Category	Subcategory	Numbers in Categories & Subcategories[a]	Percent in Categories & Subcategories[b]
Federal Groups		30	3%
	Human Resources Corporation Citizens Assemblies and Neighborhood Boards	9	1%
	Model Cities Neighborhood Planning Groups	8	1
	Urban Renewal Project Area Committees	13	1
City Groups		174	18
	City Community and Neighborhood Councils	38	3
	City Block Clubs	90	10
	Mayor's Advisory Groups	46	5
Voluntary Groups		739	79
	Patriotic and Historical Groups	15	2
	Women's Organizations	32	4
	Fellowship and Fraternal Groups	16	2
	Religious-Sponsored Organizations	39	5
	Military and Veterans' Groups	48	7
	Health, Welfare Rights, and Civil Liberties Groups	21	2
	School PTA's and Other Educational Groups	139	15
	Business and Professional Groups	27	3
	Labor Organizations	102	11
	Merchants and Trade Organizations	45	6
	Homeowners and Tenant Associations	64	8
	Privately Sponsored Economic Improvement Organizations for the Disadvantaged	7	1
	Youth Organizations	40	5
	Ethnic Groups	50	7
	Partisan Political Party Groups	14	2

[a]Numbers are estimates based on sampling. They are, moreover, subject to continuous change as new groups come into being and others go out of existence.
[b]Percentages rounded throughout table.
Source: *Organized Citizen Participation in Kansas City, Missouri* (University of Missouri—Kansas City, 1971).

6. In general, however, voluntary groups were likely to be better organized and operated with the most grass-roots initiative and the most technical competence.

As did the Atlanta study group, researchers in Kansas City, Missouri recognized the range of differences between groups *within* any categorical approach. They suggested that structural and operational factors would produce more comparative frames of reference.

DEVELOPING A CONCEPTUAL OUTLINE

The other city in the Mid-American Urban Observatory's study— Kansas City, Kansas—took on the task of designing a model for more systematic classification of different kinds of citizen groups.[6] On the basis of an extensive review of the citizen participation literature, this study group formulated the conceptual scheme depicted in Table 3-3.

Table 3-3. Conceptual Outline for Classifying Organized Citizen Groups

	Variables
The Group	1. Membership characteristics 2. Organizational structure 3. Resources
The Group's Target System	4. Target conditions 5. Target instrumentality
The Group's Program and Activities	6. Attitudinal relationship between group and instrumentality 7. Mode of Action 8. Relations with other groups 9. Beneficiaries

Source: Adapted from *Citizen Participation Groups: A Report to the National Urban Observatory* (Urban Studies Group, University of Kansas, 1970).

This outline sketches what could be assumed to be the nine major ways in which significant variations might be observed in citizen participation groups.[7] As Table 3-3 indicates, these nine areas of variation had to do with three critical elements: (1) the group itself; (2) the group's target system; and (3) the group's program and activities.

Some of these nine categories are self-explanatory. For example, what is meant by organizational and membership characteristics and resources is more or less immediately clear. At the same time, groups can differ on these attributes in many different ways.

It should be noted that the elements summarized in Table 3- 4 fit well with what has been said about independent generalizations from the Kansas City, Missouri inquiry. Federal groups and city groups there did not differ significantly on one resource variable (source of funds) but they did on the other (dimensions of resources). They also differed on both organizational structure and some membership characteristic dimensions. At the same time, both federal and city groups differed from voluntary groups on resource variables and, most probably, on many different elements of the organizational member variable.

Table 3-4. Group Characteristics within the Conceptual Outline

Variables	*Primary Analytical Components*
Membership Characteristics	1. Age
	2. Sex
	3. Religious affiliation (of all or most members)
	4. Political affiliation (of all or most members)
	5. Residence
	6. Vocation (of all or most members)
	7. Real estate ownership (for all or most members)
	8. Ethnic or genealogical background
	9. Level of income
	10. Level and type of education completed
Organization Structure	1. Degree of formality
	2. Size
	3. Longevity
	4. Affiliation with a larger organization
	5. Control procedures for membership acceptance or appointment
Resources	1. *Dimensions of resources* Amount and kind of material resources— financial resources, space and equipment
	2. *Source of funds* Funds generated from within the group or received from outside the group

Source: Adapted from *Citizen Participation Groups: A Report to the National Urban Observatory* (Urban Studies Group, University of Kansas, 1970).

The notion of the group's target system is somewhat less familiar and requires some careful definition. Target system was used to describe a group's fundamental reason for existing. Within this, the ideas of target conditions and target instrumentality are analytically separate. The first refers to a set of conditions the group wishes either (1) to change or (2) to maintain in the face of some perceived threat. Target *instrumentality* stands for those things—institutions or, perhaps, other groups or organizations—which the group has to relate to, and which stand in the way of the group's reaching its objectives. It is important to recognize that this is *not* meant to include *all* group relations with other social units. It describes only those that in a very real sense are of primary importance for the success of the group's program.

Again following the project's three-way breakdown of groups, it is clear that most federal groups had as their target conditions the whole complex of factors that add up to urban blight and its accompanying social pathologies. In such circumstances, it is hardly surprising that there was not likely to be any *single* target instrumentality (apart from the perception of some kind of a monolithic "establishment"). This is not to say, of course, that there might not be *some* instances in which the basic goal was both to redevelop *and* to maintain (e.g., "community control") and where the target instrumentalities were more focused (e.g., "institutional racism").

In these terms, many city groups and, to an even greater degree, most voluntary groups were likely to be concerned with target conditions that were more singular and more amenable to change. In line with this, the target instrumentality was at least likely to be more visible, and thus more recognizable. The character of intergroup differences on target system variables is better understood when one considers those federal groups that appeared to be more successful in gaining their objectives. As the Albuquerque, Atlanta, Baltimore, and Boston studies all concluded, this was likely to occur when the objective was very specific and the change-agent was very apparent (e.g., a tenants' group wanting a feasible change from a local housing authority).

There are, of course, many different kinds of target conditions with which citizen groups are likely to be concerned. In fleshing out its outline, the Kansas study group identified the following ten classes of conditions:

1. Public morality—(moral issues in the community)
2. Government itself—(alterations in governmental policies)
3. Education—(Condition of the school system or the learning process)
4. Community-wide well being—(cultural activities, youth programs, etc.)
5. Economic status—(financial benefits for members or their clients)

6. Anonymity—(desire to be recognized)
7. Housing—(lack of housing or housing conditions)
8. Community services—(e.g., fire or police protection, transportation)
9. Personal/family problems—(e.g., alcoholism, mental illness)
10. Environment—(conservation, preservation of the natural environment)

The nature of the group's concern should, therefore, bear some logical relationship to its target instrumentality situation. And this, together with group characteristics, should exert significant influence on the question of how the group actually functioned in attempting to reach its objectives.

In dealing with this situation—whatever it is—the group's basic strategy can involve collaboration, persuasion, or conflict tactics. Its relationships with other groups concerned with the same target situation may or may not be cooperative. Much depends, of course, on how similarly the group and its target organizations view the issues involved. There can be consensus, or when marked differences exist, there may still be a possibility that a consensus can be reached. In contrast to this situation—of ongoing but still resolvable differences—the target may refuse to recognize the issues; may refuse to recognize the group; or may flatly oppose the group's plan of action. Within the conceptual outline, this third variation has been labeled dissensus.

There are, therefore, four categories of variation for analyzing the different ways that citizen groups will try to implement their program purposes. While there ought to be a logical connection between the group's attitudinal relationship with target organizations and its mode of action (e.g., consensus and collaborative action), this may or may not be the case. It is here that more generalized attitudes of political trust and efficacy may exert significant influence on what happens. Such attitudes—in the sense that they may be modal membership characteristics of the group—should also influence the kinds of relationships that the group will develop with other organizations sharing its areas of concern.

The utility of the Kansas City design was supported by similar conclusions of Atlanta and San Diego researchers. Working independently and apart from the Kansas City inquiry, study groups in both cities came up with closely related ideas about classifying citizen groups. The Atlanta study ended by suggesting the following as the six most salient classification factors:

1. Goals and purposes of the organization.
2. Characteristics of the membership.
3. Structural characteristics of the organization.
4. Strategies and tactics used in attempting to accomplish organizational goals.
5. Degrees of influence attained by the organization.
6. The relationship of the organization to government institutions.

In a similar vein, the San Diego study suggested the following:

1. Constitution (formal organization).
2. Purpose.
3. Goals.
4. Recruitment.
5. Relations with other groups.
6. Relations with the government.

There was, therefore, much in the way of similarity and, as will be noted, most of these variables *did* have a bearing on the effectiveness of organized groups.

This is not to say that such design schemes are easy to apply. In field testing the basic design in the Kansas City, Kansas area, researchers there found that some classification variables were more immediately useful and easier to apply than others. For example, three membership characteristics of groups studied—geographic location (the residence variable) and income and education levels— were so interrelated that three very distinct kinds of citizen groups could be defined and characterized. These were: (1) inner-city groups with lower-income and lower-education members; (2) inner-city groups with middle-income and middle-education members; and (3) suburban groups with middle-income and higher-education members. These are, of course, all social class characteristics.[8]

At the same time, organizational characteristics proved to be much less discriminating—in this instance because the groups studied were so organizationally similar. Defining target conditions in precise operational terms was also very difficult. This problem involved creating broad enough categories to cover most concerns that groups will have, while simultaneously defining group interests in very specific ways. Other dilemmas involved categorizing groups with very vague and general concerns, and defining group objectives in problem-solving or other terms.

ADDITIONAL DIMENSIONS

As mentioned earlier, classification activities in study cities also involved a third focus: distinguishing between active and passive groups. The question here was the degree to which citizen groups— particularly voluntary groups—were likely to become actively involved with local public issues when they arose. This creates a whole set of subquestions that add still additional dimensions to the conceptual design for classifying groups. As Table 3- 5 indicates, such questions add two variables to the outline's section on group program and activities. While a number of cities were interested in such questions, the Milwaukee and Atlanta studies looked most directly, although somewhat differently, at this problem.

Table 3–5. Program and Activity Factors in Classifying Citizen Groups

	Variables
The Group's Program and Activities	1. Potential for group to become active about target conditions
	2. Attitudinal relationship between group and instrumentality
	3. Potential for making demands on government
	4. Mode of action
	5. Relations with other groups
	6. Beneficiaries

During the first phase of its research, the Milwaukee study group classified a large number of organizations in order to assess their potential for issue involvement during a study year, and to compare this potential with actual involvement. From records and other available sources, researchers established an initial list of more than 1000 citizen groups. This was reduced to a smaller number composed of groups that claimed to be concerned about community needs and committed to approaching local government about their concerns. The result was a list of 268 groups with an assumed potential for *future* direct involvement with local government.

This potential participation category excluded most of the city's social, cultural, fraternal, political, business, union, professional, church, and traditional social service organizations. At the same time, it included all three project categories—federal, city, and voluntary groups. Table 3- 6 describes the general character of these groups.

Table 3-6. Potentially Active Groups in a Representative Study City

Category[a]	Subcategory[b]	Numbers in Categories & Subcategories	Percentage of Total[c]
Federal		21	8%
	Required by legislation	9	3.5%
	As a result of legislation	12	4.5
City		14	5
	Initiated by City Government	8	3
	Initiated by County Government	6	2
Voluntary		233	87
	Occupational	31	11.5
	Religious	18	6.5
	Ethnic	44	16.5
	Neighborhood	40	15
	General	100	37.5

[a]City groups include both city-government-initiated and county-initiated groups within the city.

[b]Subcategories identified on the basis of group sponsorship. They can be further subdivided by specific agencies, general kind of occupation, race, and geographic location. The *general* voluntary category involves many different kinds of sponsorship and concerns with broader or more comprehensive kinds of community needs.

[c]Percentages rounded throughout the table.

Source: Adapted from *Citizen Participation: Issues and Groups* (Milwaukee Urban Observatory, 1972).

As Table 3-6 indicates, most of the city's potentially active groups were organized by citizens themselves. On the basis of sponsorship or origin, federal and city groups together made up 13 percent, and voluntary groups 87 percent of the total. While this specific pattern was not typical of every study city, it was probably quite representative. In the ten-city survey sample, almost 8 percent of those in city-problem-concerned groups belonged to government-affiliated neighborhood groups, and approximately 17 percent were members of other neighborhood organizations.[9]

The Milwaukee study's methodology further reduced the groups under consideration to the 205 that reflected more specific target condition concerns. With this revised population, the actual participation of groups was contrasted with the number that could have been involved on the basis of prestudy analysis. The results, by major issue areas, are summarized in Table 3-7. Although the full analysis of these data is too extensive to report here, a few findings most directly related to potential participation will be noted.

Table 3–7. Potential and Actual Participation in Community Issues

Issue Area[a]	Potential Group[b]	Potential Groups Actually Participating[c]	Percentage of Actual Participation[d]
Housing and Renewal	47	39	83%
Education	28	16	57
Employment and Training	17	11	65
Social Services/Welfare	16	15	95
Freeway Development	9	9	100
Law Enforcement/Police	7	5	71.5
Environment	7	5	71.5

[a]Represents 7 of 8 major community issue areas during study year.

[b]Represents number of groups identified as having a prime interest in issue area.

[c]Actual participation from newspaper coverage or questionnaire responses, with activities including adoption of official resolutions, contacts with media, authorized statements at public meetings, contacts or correspondence with officials or participation in public protests, demonstrations, or petition campaigns.

[d]Percentages rounded throughout the table.

Source: Adapted from *Citizen Participation: Issues and Groups* (Milwaukee Urban Observatory, 1972).

Table 3–7 indicates that significant proportions of groups claiming interest in a specific issue did indeed function actively when this same issue arose during the study period. It also indicates different actual-to-potential ratios for different kinds of issues. It does not, however, indicate the following:

1. In many but not all issue areas, there were more actively participating citizen groups than potential groups—in the sense that some "generally concerned" groups became involved with some specific issues. The notion of potential groups represents, therefore, the notion of a *minimum* potential.
2. Such "extra" groups were more likely to become involved with social service/welfare issues, and issues involving education, law enforcement, employment and training, and housing and renewal.
3. Such involvement probably related to the territoriality of the issue. A group with a general potential to act may not have done so if an issue arose in a neighborhood other than its own.
4. Ethnic and neighborhood factors produced the highest ratios of actual to potential issue-related participation.

By definition an interest group with a potential to act will not do so in the absence of that issue, or without the perception of an issue as relevant to broader group interests.

Atlanta researchers approached the question of potential participation from another angle. Using available records on neighborhood organizations—all voluntary groups—a sample of 270 groups was selected from geographically dispersed and racially differentiated areas. Contact officials for 185 groups were identifiable; 139 contacts were successfully made; and 103 interviews were completed. Interviews sought information about the group's purposes, activities, problem concerns, and relationships with government. Of these groups, 99 could be categorized as follows:

1. Groups located within a neighborhood but with no neighborhood focus or neighborhood concerns (30 groups—no particular nomenclature).
2. Groups that were explicitly formed for social or charitable purposes (28 groups—garden clubs and other designations).
3. Residual groups purposefully organized for one or more neighborhood-focused goals (41 groups—usually neighborhood named).

These residual groups were defined as potentially politically active and analyzed in greater detail.

As with the Milwaukee inquiry, this part of the Atlanta study is too elaborate to summarize here. Some insights can, however, be derived from Table 3-8. This table sketches the differential patterns of neighborhood groups categorized on the basis of their activities at the neighborhood level. It suggests, therefore, that "inactive groups" will rarely have relations with other groups, and such groups will not make any demands on government. "Less active groups" will have social-charitable as well as neighborhood improvement interests, and they will work somewhat more frequently with other groups. The "more active groups" will have more of a neighborhood conservation concern and still more relations with other groups.

Again, however, such a tabular outline does not indicate the more subtle but more significant differences between groups. In this Atlanta study, these included the following:

1. "More active groups" put greater emphasis on their communication functions—representation of their community's interests, making known the needs of the neighborhood, and informing their memberships.
2. "Less active groups" made different kinds of demands on local

Table 3–8. Neighborhood Groups in a Study City

Activity Level[a]	*Inactive*	*Less Active*	*More Active*
Number of Groups	12 (29.3%)	9 (21.9%)	20 (48.8%)
Purposes[b]	Neighborhood improvement (83%)	Neighborhood improvement (67%)	Neighborhood conservation (60%)
	Neighborhood conservation (17%)	Social and charitable (33%)	Neighborhood improvement (40%)
Other Group Relations[c]	Few affiliations	More affiliations	Most affiliations
Public Agency Relations[d]	Very few relations	No relations	Very few relations
Demands on local government	None	Some	Some

[a]Activity-level categories determined from the *relative* number of specific neighborhood activities reported by group spokesmen.

[b]Neighborhood improvement defined as concerns with beautification, area development, and specific neighborhood needs. In contrast, neighborhood conservation defined as concerns for maintenance of area's physical environment and general welfare.

[c]Generalizations from *relative* number of relations reported by group spokesmen.

[d]Generalizations from *relative* number of relations reported by group spokesmen.

Source: Adapted from *General Survey of Organized Citizen Participation* (Atlanta Urban Observatory, 1970).

government. They "asked" or "requested" city agencies for things like street resurfacing or neighborhood cleanup. Their own reported activities seemed to have little relationship to the kinds of demands they made.

3. "More active groups" evidenced a "doing" orientation in registering voters, assisting tenants groups, starting litigation, developing a community plan, and so on. They dealt with all available levels of government, lobbied, and made more contacts with elected officials and policy bodies.

4. "More active groups," as described here, were not distinguishable on the basis of race, but most tended to be found in upper-class neighborhoods.

On the basis of these and other situational factors, Atlanta researchers concluded that the relative presence or absence of factors that were or could be disruptive to established neighborhood patterns would largely determine the degree to which such groups would relate aggressively to local government. They found that "inactive groups" were concentrated in areas that were relatively well-insulated from redevelopment and racial impacts, while the "more active" groups were those whose neighborhoods were in the direct path of such social-change events. The most volatile bodies of all were not even in the study sample. These were ad hoc citizen groups, "instant organizations" formed at the neighborhood level in reaction to re-zoning proposals or other triggering events.

To a considerable degree, the more specific Milwaukee classification data supported the general Atlanta conclusions. The kinds of issues that activated most potentially active groups in Mil-waukee involved both physical change and social conflict. In that study, inner-city locations were characterized as "path of social change" areas—areas with high population density, less than adequate housing resources, urban renewal demolition activities without prompt reconstruction, extensive freeway construction, relatively high crime rates, relatively low income levels, and poor educational attainment rates. Under such circumstances, a positive relationship between social-change events and the development of citizen groups concerned about change was hardly surprising. For the "new citizen participa-tion," therefore, the locational factor may be a critical variable.

CONCLUSIONS

Classifying citizen groups is, to understate the matter, both difficult and complex. Although membership and other group variables are likely to determine the group's agenda, and the character of rela-tionships with target organizations may predict the strategy and tactics for group activities, the nature of the group's target may ultimately determine the feasibility of its objectives.

As the Kansas City design suggests, groups can be classified along various dimensions of these elements. And, at least implicitly, a group's effectiveness will involve an appropriate set of interactions ·among these variables. In adding notions of potentiality to the de-sign, the Milwaukee and Atlanta studies (1) reinforced the assump-tion that all kinds of citizen groups are able to function politically; and (2) established that group activity is clearly associated with situational change. At the very least, therefore, *active* citizen partici-pation should be seen as a dynamic process within a social-change context.

NOTES

1. See page 136 of the Bollens-Schmandt citation (n. 1) to Chapter 1.
2. For purposes of this study, therefore, the term "community action groups"

is being used more broadly, and it is not restricted to those groups defined by the Community Action Program of the Office of Economic Opportunity.

3. Although the initial working committee of project designers and study directors was primarily interested in such "newer groups" coming out of federal urban programming, the intent of the project always assumed the need for a reasonably comprehensive approach that would include longer-established and more "natural" community organizations.

4. For purposes of simplicity and convenience, individual city studies are referred to in short form—e.g., as the Atlanta study. In each instance, such a reference should imply all of the project reports for that city—as outlined in Appendix B.

5. This is, of course, inherent in the term parapolitical.

6. One element in the project's original design called for individual Observatories to take responsibility for a piece of specific and more in-depth work.

7. The citizen participation literature is loaded with many diverse classification schemes, models, and paradigms. These differ primarily in terms of specific research objectives or analytical purposes. For a promising typology of citizen participation programs, see Richard L. Cole, *Citizen Participation and the Urban Policy Process* (Lexington, Mass.: D. C. Heath, 1974). Cole's typology employs three gradations of citizen influence and three levels of program scope as major variables for assessment of (some) participant characteristics, trust and satisfaction.

8. As used here, the term inner-city is equivalent to center-city (as contrasted with suburban municipalities).

9. These proportions are drawn from original (not recoded) data in the Citizens' Attitude Survey's tabulations.

Chapter Four

Perceptions of Community Issues

PRIMARY ISSUES IN STUDY CITIES

Citizen participation investigators in Observatory cities used issue analysis to identify groups that were likely to relate to city government. They examined newspaper accounts of controversial community issues and interviewed officials and others knowledgeable about local affairs. Although an emphasis on one or the other of these two methods produced somewhat different results, most studies found a relatively high level of agreement on basic issues.

There was, moreover, considerable overlap among study cities. For example, six cities reported the issue-analysis results shown in Table 4-1. As this table indicates, issues overlapped to a considerable degree, both across cities and within cities. In the first instance, issues all concerned problems of planning and development in cities trying to provide services with an increasingly eroded tax base. In this sense, therefore, such issues were probably typical of both study cities and cities more generally. Although not included in the table, San Diego study conclusions indicated that city's media-reported issues as dealing primarily with urban planning and education problems.[1]

SOME NECESSARY QUALIFICATIONS

It does not follow, of course, that all such issues were necessarily of major concern to most citizens.[2] For example, media coverage of school issues having to do with parent participation or community

Table 4-1.   Basic Issues in Representative Study Cities

Issues	Atlanta	Boston	Denver	Kansas City, Missouri	Milwaukee	Nashville
Housing[a]	X	X	X	X	X	X
Freeway Construction		X		X	X	X
Mass Transit	X		X			
Planning and Zoning			X			X
Race Relations	X		X	X		
Taxes and Revenue			X	X	X	
Education[b]	X	X	X	X	X	
Urban Renewal		X				X
Welfare Rights	X				X	
Citizen Participation[c]			X		X	X

[a]Includes tenants rights, low-income housing, project locations, and construction strikes.

[b]Includes questions of school integration, educational quality, parent participation, and community control.

[c]Includes issues within Model Cities and other federally funded programs.

Sources: Adapted from Atlanta, Boston, Denver, Kansas City, Missouri, Milwaukee, and Nashville studies (see Appendix B).

control might suggest that these were matters of very widespread concern in citizen participation study cities. Data from the ten-city Attitude Survey indicated otherwise. For the most part, the great majorities in these study cities were satisfied with the degree to which they could influence school policies. Between 68 and 84 percent of the adults interviewed felt they had the right amount of say in their school systems. Only about 3 percent suggested a need for increased parent participation in the educational process.[3]

   On the other hand, specific cities may have highly particularized broad-based concerns that *are* reflected as community-wide issues. For example, as the Albuquerque study noted, environmental matters were likely to be paramount in that city. While this study cited a wide range of issues about which citizen groups were concerned, the most frequently mentioned involved events that were likely to have a perceptible environmental impact. Similarly—and recognizing that issues vary with time—in Atlanta during 1969-70, the major issue from the vantage point of the larger community may well have been the "hippie movement." Although omitted from the table because of its somewhat unique character, this issue had to do with the large concentrations of "new life-style" youth in near-downtown areas. Both media analysis and interviews concluded that this was a significant issue. In this instance, attitude survey data were more than substantiating. Although not a matter of much relevance in other study cities, the issue was of major concern to large numbers of Atlantans.[4]

In a still more significant sense, the major issues that concerned citizen groups overlapped in terms of critical dimensions common to two or more issues. For example, there is little doubt that Table 4-1, as presented, very greatly minimizes the significance of race-relations problems. Although this is cited as a basic issue in three of the six cities represented, the table's format hides the degree to which race was a critical variable in other issue areas. In reporting their interview data, Atlanta researchers noted that race relations permeated discussions with officials and other knowledgeables. For the majority of those interviewed, it was a fundamental theme around which a number of other issues revolved. This was so in spite of the fact that the city had not experienced any major racial incident during the study period. In reporting their media data, Atlanta researchers concluded that about three out of four issue-oriented groups (58 of 78) were concerned with educational, welfare, housing, and police problems that were *racial* in character.[5]

Study personnel in Kansas City, Missouri reached a similar conclusion in analyzing expert views in that city. Extracting all issues that clearly involved significant civil rights or race conflicts and "converting them" to race relations issues, they found that such issues were as frequently mentioned as all other issues combined. And almost twice as many citizen groups were associated with such race-relations issues.[6]

Since five other study cities besides Atlanta had black populations similar to or proportionately greater than Kansas City, Missouri, it is reasonable to assume that knowledgeables in these cities were also seeing many housing and urban redevelopment issues as having either racial components or racial overtones. Analysis of case studies in most cities supports such an assumption. In a very real way, therefore, the issues in Table 4-1 could be recast into (1) those that *undoubtedly* had significant racial elements attached to them; and (2) those that may or may not—depending on the specific situation—have had race-relations overtones. Housing, urban renewal, education, and welfare rights are issues that were unequivocally in the first category.

As the Milwaukee study indicated, these were the issues that were likely to activate the greatest proportions of potentially concerned citizen groups. These same issues also had a capacity to attract ethnically conscious or neighborhood-focused kinds of organizations. As far as the other issues were concerned—freeway construction, mass transit, planning and zoning, taxes and revenue, and citizen participation—these also frequently involved more than racial overtones. A large number of case studies within the citizen participation study demonstrated this.

THE POLITICAL RELEVANCE OF ISSUES

The simple frequency of an issue's being mentioned—in media coverage or during interview situations—did not, therefore, say very much about the relative *political* importance of that issue in a given city. To find out what the more pressing and more politically significant issues were, researchers in Denver asked their informants to rank the major public-policy problems they had identified in order of importance. In this particular instance, the eight knowledgeables included two councilmen, two city administrators, two university faculty members, and two other citizens not identified with the first three pairs. The results of this inquiry are outlined in Table 4- 2.

   With this method, mass transit, housing, and planning and zoning emerged as the three most significant problems. In an attempt to isolate the one issue most likely to stimulate citizen activity, respondents were asked: "In terms of citizen participation, around which issues do citizen goups most frequently coalesce?" The unanimous response was around zoning.

   On the basis of both media analysis (looking into the record) and media monitoring (analysis of subsequent coverage), Denver researchers arrived at the following conclusions:

1.   The *initial* review of the media did not bear out the respondent consensus that zoning was an important issue. The inquiry had apparently gone too far back in time.
2.   Subsequent media review—closer to the time of interviewing— fully corroborated the collective judgment of respondents.
3.   Zoning appeared to be very important to the citizenry at large, and the other issues that respondents rated as important seemed to be validated by newspaper coverage.
4.   During subsequent mayoral and councilmanic election campaigns, *all nine* problems previously identified by respondents became major campaign issues. Some of these issues were, of course, given a political twist.[7]

In addition to buttressing the validity of the project's issue-identification approach, the Denver results indicated that issues looked at in study cities were politically very relevant. It also suggested: (1) that politically sensitive people will view citizen participation in terms of *current* issues: and (2) that these same people will define organized citizen action to include *more* than formally established continuing groups.

Table 4-2. Significance of Issues in a Study City

Respondent	Mass Transit	Race	Employ-ment	Education	Taxes & Revenue	Environ-ment	Participa-tion Communi-cation	Planning & Zoning	Housing
Councilman 1	5	3	2.5	1.5	2	1			
Councilman 2			4	3			3		5
Administrator 1 City	5				3				4
Administrator 2 City	3	1	2	2	1			5	4
University 1	5	3			2				4
University 2	4	3						1	5
Other Citizen 1		3	3	1	1			9	
Other Citizen 2	2							9	2
Totals[a]	24	13	11.5	7.5	9	1	3	24	24

[a]Issues assigned values on weighted bases of 5, 4, 3, 2, and 1, according to the order offered by respondents during interview. If respondent listed an issue as number one, that issue was valued at 5; the second ranked issue was valued at 4; and so on until the last issue listed was valued at 1.

Source: Adapted from *Citizen Power and Participation—Groups, Issues, and Impact—Within the Political Culture of Denver* (Denver Urban Observatory, 1972).

Although their approach was less elaborate, Atlanta researchers uncovered similar phenomena. Political officials on this study's interview panel saw zoning issues as among the most significant of the city's problems. And, as far as citizen participation was concerned, they viewed zoning as politically volatile in producing organized citizen groups throughout the city. As reported in Chapter 3, the Atlanta study found such ad hoc citizen groups to be among the most politically aggressive of the city's neighborhood bodies. The political significance of this issue was further validated by subsequent mayoral statements about zoning as the city problem most needing to be researched.[8]

RELEVANCE TO THE MEDIA

The precise degree to which expert opinions and newspaper accounts agree on the issues depends on how one looks at the matter. As noted, Denver researchers concluded from media review that knowledgeable informants could identify the issues that were subsequently relevant during a political campaign. Working in the other direction—from an extensive newspaper analysis to interviews with officials and other informed sources—Atlanta researchers discovered that their respondents did not identify any new problems that had not already been covered to some degree by the local press.

There may, however, be some significant differences when more specific issues are evaluated, and there will almost certainly be differences in emphasis. For example, during the study period in Kansas City, Missouri, the press and experts agreed on only six of the ten specific issues most frequently noted. Of these, the two most frequently reported by the press were those the experts ranked at the bottom. In this instance, study analysts speculated that the press tended to focus more on economic problems—on the city's financial situation and its economic well-being. While experts also evidenced such concerns, they emphasized other issues of more interest to the average citizen.[9]

It may have been, of course, that many community problems—among them the broad issues being studied in this project—were so complex and so frequently localized that they were not readily amenable to adequate press coverage. The citizen groups involved, particularly those functioning over an extended period of time, may not have been continuously visible in any dramatic way that would have made them particularly newsworthy.[10] However, even when issues were specific, visible, and citywide in their implications, coverage may still have been less than some policy-makers would have liked. For example, in assessing newspaper coverage of nine major issues and related issue-concerned citizen organizations in their study, Nashville researchers concluded that very little press coverage was evaluational, and depth analysis was virtually nonexistent. Over half of this study's citizen group press reports involved relatively obscure coverage, and any emphasis that did exist was on group relationships with government.[11]

RECOGNITION OF CITIZEN GROUPS

As a number of the project's studies pointed out, citizen groups tended to be disproportionately concerned with certain kinds of issues. For some issues, therefore, a large number of groups were involved, and many of these were groups organized at the community or neighborhood level. This raises the general question of how well city officials are able to identify and differentiate specific citizen organizations.

Project investigators suggested that when broad public issues were under discussion, city officials, as well as the press, found it difficult to identify any key citizen groups. Among other things, this might have been due to the enlarged numbers of organized groups in many cities.[12] As the Denver study reported, that city's middle-class communities have demonstrated heightened group activity during the sixties, and minority group activity has also increased.[13] In Baltimore, another study city, neighborhood organizations are said to have increased from 163 in 1956 to 261 in 1970. While such "community revolutions" may not have occurred in every study city, it is probable that they had in most.

Officials and community leaders were, of course, able to name definite groups when specific public issues of some consequence were involved. While such groups were also likely to have had some press visibility, they were not necessarily the organizations that had received the most continuing kinds of coverage. As Table 4-3—drawn from the Kansas City, Missouri study—demonstrates, the press and local experts did not always agree on the organizations that were most relevantly involved with major community issues. Although, in this instance, both press and experts were evaluating the same community, it is apparent that they were seeing rather different sets of organizational actors as significant. This was due, of course, to the fact that they were seeing some community issues as differentially relevant.

For the most part, press coverage dealt with labor, business, and professional organizations as issue-involved, with less

Table 4–3.   Issue-Related Organizations in a Study City

Frequency Rankings

Press		Experts	
1. Iron Workers #10	39	1. Panthers, Soul Inc., and "Militants"	18
2. Builders Association	29	2. Chamber of Commerce	4
3. Panthers, Soul Inc.	21	3. Labor	4
4. Painters District Council #3	14	4. Commission on Human Relations	4
5. Teamsters 541	10	5. Westport-Townoke Community Council	3
6. Lumberman's Association	9	6. Retail Merchants Association	3
7. Kansas City Federation of Teachers	9	7. Mid-City Congress	3
8. Chamber of Commerce	8	8. Model Cities Planning Groups	3
9. Kansas City Committee for School Levy	6	9. Citizen Association	2
10. Metropolitan Citizens for Education	5	10. Home Builders Association	2

Source: *Organized Citizen Participation in Kansas City, Missouri* (University of Missouri—Kansas City, 1971).

frequent mention of the kinds of community-level interest groups that are now normally associated with the term citizen participation. Experts, on the other hand, were more likely to identify "militants" and other racially or community concerned groups, while still recognizing other kinds of civic organizations. To some degree, this difference might have been due to a study methodology that asked experts for more specific information about citizen participation. It is more likely, however, that the difference represented the heightened consciousness that officials would inevitably have as the natural result of more direct relationships with citizens and their group leaderships.

The overall significance of press coverage is difficult to appraise. Researchers in San Diego placed more reliance on interviews with knowledgeable informants, because of what they perceived to be a newspaper tendency to underreport activities of that city's minority groups.[14] If, however, such underreporting existed in San Diego, it is just as likely that overreporting would have been the case in those study cities where the local press was highly critical of the mayor or the city administration.[15]

As the Baltimore study report asserted, the kind of participation that has most concerned city officials in recent years has involved citizen intervention in the operations of city agencies—participation in the processes of delivering public goods and services.[16] If this is so, then agency administrators ought to have had somewhat greater—or at least somewhat different—understandings of organized citizen groups than elected officials. Although not a matter of general study, the Milwaukee report does note some differences in this regard. Researchers there reported that appointed officials were more likely than elected officials to identify neighborhood, ethnic, or other special-purpose citizen groups as being among the organizations they called on for advice or assistance. In the same vein, appointed officials were more aware of the groups involved in specific issues, and more able or willing to identify the groups they saw as inhibiting agency objectives.

However, both kinds of officials—elected and appointed—tended to seek advice or assistance primarily from long-established and more prestigious business, labor, or community organizations. In relating to organizations demanding change, both generally found suspect those citizen groups that did not or would not use established vehicles for contacting them.[17] The Albuquerque and San Diego studies also suggest that city officials reflect a natural preference for dealing with citizen groups in more, rather than less, controlled circumstances. As the latter study noted, on any given issue, officials will want to work with a single group—preferably one that is both established and familiar to them.[18]

Some groups of this sort were, of course, structurally tied to city government. While many project researchers case-studied groups involved in model cities and economic opportunity programs, this did not represent a specific general study focus. It may be sufficient, therefore, to indicate here that such structured relationships could and did produce a range of quite different results. For example, while citizen participation in the Model Cities program was one of the most controversial issues in the Milwaukee study, it was a matter of relatively minor concern in Atlanta. In other study cities, it fell, as an issue, between these two extremes.[19]

CONCLUSIONS

As is usually the case, specific situations will determine how visible and how viable citizen groups will be in relation to community issues and in relation to local governments. As noted in Chapter 3, Atlanta researchers reported that its city's purely voluntary neighborhood groups varied widely in their active relationships with government. Their more detailed analysis concluded that virtually all groups that could be classified as politically active were in areas of the city where physical or social changes were threatening disruption of established neighborhood patterns. For the most part, these Atlanta groups were located in upper- upper-middle- and middle-class neighborhoods.

In Denver as in Atlanta, such middle-class activism was triggered by proposed rezonings and other kinds of neighborhood transition. Greater activism in the inner city, as the Milwaukee study demonstrated, resulted from neighborhoods in the path of other kinds of social change, primarily from freeway construction, urban renewal demolition, and forced relocation. Confronted with such changes—and given the already apparent consequences of high densities, inadequate housing, and other social dislocations—it was hardly surprising that inner-city groups escalated their demands on the nearest available government. For most study cities, therefore, the "new citizen participation" involved heavy situational loadings of both middle-class and inner-city activism.

NOTES

1. As generalizations, and not as summarized data, these conclusions were not included in Table 4-1.
2. Among others, Jackson and Slade have established that "city participation

activists" and the "community at large" can differ significantly in their policy orientations toward the community. In general terms, citizens of the community at large most frequently and most relevantly see the community as a provider of services, while citizen participants, with their more structured orientations, tend to view the city as an agent of community change. For a full analysis of these and related matters, see John S. Jackson III and William L. Slade, "Citizen Participation, Democratic Representation, and Survey Research," *Urban Affairs Quarterly* 9 (September 1973): 57-89.

3. These data and conclusions can be found in the reports cited in note 6 of Chapter 1.

4. In addition to the above, see *General Survey of Organized Citizen Participation* (Atlanta Urban Observatory, Atlanta, 1970); John D. Hutcheson, Jr. and Frank X. Steggert, *Organized Citizen Participation in Urban Areas* (Center for Research in Social Change, Emory University, Atlanta, 1970); and Tim C. Ryles, *Citizen Attitudes toward Public Policies and Political Authorities in Atlanta* (Atlanta Urban Observatory, Atlanta, 1971).

5. See *General Survey of Organized City Participation* (Atlanta Urban Observatory, Atlanta, 1970). Referred to hereafter as Atlanta study report.

6. See *Organized City Participation in Kansas City, Missouri* (Mid-America Urban Observatory, Kansas City, Missouri, 1971). Referred to hereafter as Kansas City, Missouri study report.

7. See *Citizen Participation in Denver: Volume III* (Denver Urban Observatory, Denver, 1972). Referred to hereafter as Denver study report.

8. See Atlanta study report.

9. See Kansas City, Missouri study report.

10. The need for such visibility through publicity—for relatively powerless citizen groups—is discussed in Hutcheson and Steggert, op. cit., pp. 121-125. Their analysis derives from Michael Lipsky, "Protest as a Political Resource," *American Political Science Review* 62 (December 1968).

11. See *Beyond the Ballot: Organized Citizen Participation in Metropolitan Nashville* (Urban Observatory of Metropolitan Nashville University Centers, Nashville, 1971). Referred to hereafter as Nashville study report.

12. Most analysts of the new citizen participation have accepted the claim that the sixties involved "more people in more organized groups for more purposes than ever before." See Daniel Bell and Virginia Held, "The Community Revolution," *The Public Interest* 16 (Summer 1969): 142-177.

13. See Denver study report.

14. See *Citizen Participation Groups in San Diego* (Urban Observatory of San Diego, San Diego, 1971). Referred to hereafter as San Diego study report.

15. From a subjective but somewhat knowledgeable vantage point, the author

would contend that such overreporting was characteristic of such citizen group activity in Milwaukee.

16. See *Survey of Organized Citizen Participation in Baltimore* (Baltimore Urban Observatory, Inc., Baltimore, 1970). Referred to hereafter as Baltimore study report.

17. See *Citizen Participation: Issues and Groups, Milwaukee, Wisconsin, 1969* (Milwaukee Urban Observatory, Milwaukee, 1972). Referred to hereafter as Milwaukee study report.

18. See San Diego study report.

19. These are, of course, personal conclusions based on review and analysis of all the various city study reports.

Chapter Five

Problems of Group Effectiveness

ASSESSING GROUP EFFECTIVENESS

Few research tasks in recent years have been potentially less productive than evaluation of programs and organizational effectiveness.[1] The Urban Observatory citizen participation project assumed, however, that study cities would have to build some appraisals of group effectiveness into their research strategies. Thus the assessment of effectiveness was posited as one study goal. At the same time, no specific method for such evaluations was prescribed.[2] It was assumed that approaches would involve perceptions of organizational effectiveness—from the vantage points of city officials, community knowledgeables, and group leaders. It was also assumed that the various designs would involve some more controlled kinds of analysis. Both assumptions proved correct, and the general results of such findings are summed up below.

VIEWS OF OFFICIALS AND OTHER KNOWLEDGEABLES

As far as perceptions of city officials and community knowledgeables were concerned, an initial safe generalization would be that these informants generally saw citizen groups as having some impact or effect. For example, members of the Atlanta interview panel considered such groups as markedly effective in having a direct impact on specific aspects of public policy. According to this response pattern, there would probably be many more rezonings without protests by organized citizen groups; urban renewal decisions were being determined by inner city-groups; and welfare-rights groups were functioning with "high impact and lots of influence." Community clubs were characterized as influential, and neighborhood advisory bodies were credited with having had a "dramatic influence" on the Housing Authority.[3]

Some groups were, of course, viewed as ineffective—either because of their targets or because of the nature of their demands. The most notable instance of perceived failure had to do with the inability of the community's many educationally concerned groups to have any influence on what they saw as a recalcitrant school system. City advisory groups were characterized as making "usually innocuous demands." More importantly, perhaps, most of these local experts indicated, in one way or another, the relation of effectiveness to specificity of demand. Various respondents reported that "citizens get impact on specifics," and others attributed the success of organized citizen participation to the existence of so many "single-purpose groups."[4]

In Atlanta—as well as in some other study cities—perceptions of groups were inextricably tied to their involvements in specific issues. And this perception seemed to be only partly related to the citizen participation study's issue-oriented methods. Neighborhood groups were frequently recognized because they emerged as visible during crisis situations. In Atlanta, the critical issue of race relations involved major local black civil-rights groups that functioned, as coalition bodies, only in times of perceived crisis. At the level of public visibility, such groups were not formal organizations at all. And yet, in certain crisis-oriented circumstances they emerged in a very visible way.[5]

The assumption that crisis-oriented organized citizen opinion will significantly influence political decisions was verified in a related Atlanta study. In looking at citizen involvement with zoning issues, it was determined that the Board of Aldermen did indeed listen to citizens who showed up at zoning hearings. At least, as Table 5-1 indicates, the weight of citizen opposition bore a strong relationship to the Board's action.

Cases that had no opposition were approved 81 percent of the time, while those with large opposition groups at hearings were approved in only 29 percent of the cases. As subsequent analysis indicated, cases were not very dissimilar in character, and the content of arguments did not vary much from case to case. Of all the factors examined, size of opposition bore a greater relationship to the final outcome than any other factor.[6]

Table 5–1. Citizen Opposition and Zoning Decisions in a Study
City

Number of Citizens in Opposition	Cases Approved		Cases Denied		Cases Deferred	
	Number	*Percent*	*Number*	*Percent*	*Number*	*Percent*
None	30	81%	5	14%	2	5%
1–10	21	58	8	22	7	20
More than 10	9	29	15	48	7	23

Source: *Zoning Problems in Atlanta: Two Studies of Policy, Practice and Community Acceptance and Their Problem-Solving Applications* (Atlanta Urban Observatory, 1972).

Apart from crisis and public-visibility situations, perceptions of group effectiveness were likely to be significantly affected by more general attitudes toward organized citizen participation (Table 5- 2). Although the Atlanta study may or may not be typical, it is clear that some valued the concept more than others.[7]

Conclusions from these viewpoints are basically self-evident, and profiles are relatively easy to draw. The very familiarity of these perspectives suggests that informants in this one city may well have been representing the modal range of views to be found in study cities and cities more generally.[8] For the most part, spokesmen were implying (1) the need to locate and utilize more leadership at the grass-roots level; and (2) the need to involve those who historically have been excluded. A jaundiced reaction might see this opinion syndrome as quite conservative. A more supportive reaction might see it as illustrating a concern for traditional concepts of representative government.

In the context of another study city—Milwaukee—the judgment of local government officials that organized citizen groups were effective was reduceable to the overall belief that they helped with the development of community issues. In this sense, citizen group activity (1) reinforced official viewpoints; (2) demonstrated community support for established policy positions; or (3) encouraged broader community understanding of issues. It was in this somewhat restricted sense, therefore, that groups were seen as affecting policy postures. At the same time, detailed case histories in this study indicated that official positions did change on all the prime issues that were analyzed. The effect of citizen group activity was, however, somewhat obscured by local government's need to follow federal guidelines or direct and indirect possibilities that federal program funds might otherwise be withheld.[9]

Table 5-2. Expert Views of Organized Citizen Participation in a Study City

Officials[a]		*Expressed Views*[b]
"Believers"	Concept Good—	It is important to have avenues for citizens to express themselves both individually and collectively. Opinions and interests of citizens *must* be taken into consideration. The involved citizen is a good citizen. It is necessary to bring this kind of middle class virtue to groups not in this tradition.
	Reservations—	Are inner-city citizens able to run community development programs? Group representatives need to be chosen on the basis of legal and democratic processes. Citizens ought not to have equal responsibility and elected officials must have the final decision. It's too early to determine how far you can go with this. The political process must be protected.
"Disbelievers"	Reservations—	Most groups involve two or three cliques trying to diminate the entire group. There are too many problems of what to accomplish and how and who is to lead in what direction. It provides too many avenues for seeking personal recognition. It leads to raising of issues to justify the group's existence.
Knowledgeables[c]		
"Believers"	Concept Good—	It represents the life blood of the community. It is one of the most healthy things that our society has witnessed in the last decade. Its real relevance is at the program planning level. Citizen inputs are functional when ground rules and reciprocal responsibilities are understood.
	Reservations—	Permanent citizen participation structures are probably not necessary. Citizens are never really active or involved except in times of crisis.

[a]Officials were two aldermen, two city executives in top management positions, and a county management executive (4 whites and 1 black).

[b]Views are adapted from interview-records.

[c]Knowledgeables included two university administrators, two community agency executives, and a public affairs journalist (5 whites).

Source: *General Survey of Organized Citizen Participation*, Atlanta Urban Observatory, 1970.

In Milwaukee, as in Albuquerque and San Diego, the question of effectiveness perceptions was further contaminated by the general expectations officials had about the ways in which government ought to be approached and the kind of demands that ought to be made. In this sense, therefore, the "effectiveness" perceptions of officials were likely to reflect their evaluations of the "correctness" of the group's total behavior pattern. If this was so, then the effective group was more likely to be the one that generally conformed to such patterns of expectation.

In this context, and defining effectiveness as successful resolution of group concerns and communication with political officials as the necessary instrument, the Albuquerque study concluded that effective issue-concerned groups had the following characteristics:

1. They were cooperative rather than conflict-oriented.
2. They had already assembled some economic and political resources.
3. They had engaged in prior successful negotiations.
4. They used their information in simple and forthright ways.
5. They made demands that could be politically acceded to.[10]

Given these circumstances and turning them around, it is not surprising that officials would see effective citizen groups as those stable and established organizations that did their homework well and presented their cases in a direct spirit-of-cooperation way.

Given the ability to choose the groups to deal with about community issues, officials would naturally want to work with "effective groups," so defined. In its analysis of community cases, the San Diego study found a predictable pattern.

1. Officials worked closely with only one group in a community.
2. In each case, the group's leadership represented an above-average income level in the community.[11]
3. Such spokesmen groups were thought to be more conservative than other segments of the community.
4. Such groups were familiar in the sense that they had organizational ties with government or had worked with government before.
5. The citizens involved usually worked through their councilmen in trying to resolve the issue.

So city officials did develop expectations about how groups should act and, to a great degree, this involved the absence of conflict. In this kind of a more limited negotiating arena, the variable that seemed to determine success was the ability of the group's leadership to gather community support while damping down intergroup conflict to the degree that it did not become publicly visible.[12]

To some extent, therefore, this preference orientation explains the often hostile posture of city officials toward groups that seem to be openly and deliberately conflict prone. And yet, as many "protest politics" analysts suggest, the visibility that such public-arena conflicts can produce may be a valuable asset to those relatively powerless groups that lack other more conventional resources. The Atlanta study—in its partial focus on comparative case studies—considered this and related variables in evaluating organizational effectiveness. In studying three citizen organizations with uniquely different membership characteristics, it was found that the two "relatively powerless" groups involved were able to use third-party supports and media attention as means for at least partial attainment of immediate objectives. Both groups seemed to have turned in this direction because they were not very readily able to use the personal-contact (with agencies and officials) approach available and familiar to middle- and upper-middle-class organizations.[13] And as the Boston study found, conflict tactics can often be employed with meaningful effect if later-phase activities are partially accommodating or compromising in character.[14]

OTHER DIMENSIONS

Most community groups were not continuously involved with conflict situations. For most, the more normal course involved working away at neighborhood development concerns. In somewhat different ways, the Kansas City (Kansas), Cleveland, and Baltimore studies all treated questions of group effectiveness in this more stable context.

The Cleveland study was somewhat unique in focusing on a single community, which was black, relatively stable, and devoid of any federal groups.[15] In one sense, all of the service-oriented city and voluntary groups in this community had to be appraised as *ineffective*. Resident participation was so minimal that it could not be quantified. As a result, membership in any organization at any time was used as an indicator of citizen involvement. With such a gross grouping variable, the usual class-participation factors were not discriminating. The factors that most influenced residents to become clients of the available service organizations were length of residence and home ownership in the community.

At the awareness level, residents in Cleveland were more familiar with the community's multiservice organizations. For the minority that participated as clients, some evidence indicated that greater involvement was related to opportunity for participation in organizational decisionmaking. On an overall basis, however, community organizations were seen as ineffectual because they had no real capacities to affect the community-decay and community-improvement concerns that were their manifest goals. They were, moreover, cut off from any significant contacts with the local political system.

In sharp contrast to the Cleveland inquiry, field research in Kansas City, Kansas dealt *only* with groups that could be classified as successful. From standardized interviews with the active leaderships of 33 community groups throughout the metropolitan area, study personnel were able to classify 24 groups as perceiving themselves as either unsuccessful, somewhat successful, successful, or very successful. As might be anticipated and as Table 5- 3 indicates, perceptions were differentially distributed on a class-location basis.

Table 5- 3. Leader Perceptions of Group Success in a Study City

Category	Number in Category	Perceived as Unsuccessful	Perceived as Somewhat Successful	Perceived as Successful	Perceived as Very Successful
Suburban, with Middle-Income, Higher-Education Members	10	0	2	1	7
Inner-City, with Middle-Income, Middle-Education Members	5	0	1	1	3
Inner-City, with Lower-Income, Lower-Education Members	9	4	2	0	3

Source: *Adapted from Citizen Participation Groups: A Report to the National Urban Observatory* (Urban Studies Group, University of Kansas, 1970).

In each instance, perceptions of success were aligned with the degrees to which different categories reported different proportions of internal, external, and financial problems. In this study's comparative design, therefore, a measure for determining "unqualified success" was developed. Groups were rated as successful only if they were perceived by their leaderships as very successful and if they reflected less than the average number of problems for the groups being studied. Twelve groups met both criteria, and four were selected for case analysis. Three were inner-city groups, with two of the three in the middle-income category, and one was a suburban group.

Case analyses of these successful groups—all varying in size, location, income, and target concern—revealed some clear behavioral commonalities. The following appeared to be most explanatory:

1. A significant proportion of each group's activities was initiated by a small dedicated leadership cadre within the larger, more general membership structure.
2. This leadership cadre studied the structure and operations of the target agency to learn how the system worked.
3. The organization made direct contacts—letters, calls or visits—to those officials who had the authority to act.[16]

Such behaviors were very similar to findings in a number of other study cities.

The Baltimore study also engaged in a comparative analysis of organizational behavior within community-level citizen groups. Seven organizations were selected as representative from a larger list of the city's neighborhood-based citizen groups. Intensive case studies, including direct observations, of these seven revealed four organizations that represented most of the major variations in the city's styles of citizen participation.

In a general, sequencing way, the principal research results of the Baltimore analysis can be summarized as follows:

1. Contrary to one major school of thought, internal rivalries within groups did *not* produce many projects, proposals, or demands—i.e., a full organizational agenda. Such conflict and competition within groups were associated with the *absence* of a full agenda.
2. Such an empty agenda—having few specific items of business about which to make organizational decisions—seemed to be the most troublesome problem a community group could have.
3 Government groups—particularly federal groups—suffered from this problem, in having less extensive agendas of projects, proposals, and demands than voluntary groups.
4. The nature of government programs—efforts to achieve general, long-term, and often ill-defined goals—was probably responsible, since most voluntary groups had rather specific and immediate program objectives.
5. The problem of government groups was complicated by the centralized city-wide direction of program elements, and thus programs and neighborhood units were organizationally separated.

6. The problem was aggravated still further when government groups tended to employ professional staffs that were more concerned about organizational problems than neighborhood problems.
7. While group leaders tried a variety of things to compensate for empty agendas, these were likely to be poor substitues for problem identification and the resources to attempt solutions.
8. In addition to the empty agenda situation, neighborhood groups tended to suffer from clique-formation conflicts that came from prior group attachments and friendships among members.
9. Consolidation of groups into larger regional confederations could possibly have helped with this situation by focusing attention away from intragroup concerns.
10. Such confederation might also have provided the means through which groups could have acquired more in the way of problem-oriented staff support.[17]

Once again, elements in this set of conclusions and observations were generally substantiated in other city studies.

CONCLUDING REMARKS

At this point it would be redundant to indicate how other studies—such as those in Atlanta, Boston, and Milwaukee—reinforced aspects of the Baltimore study's results. As has already been noted, this summary's focus is on common results, and not on each of the separate city studies. Individual cities are cited primarily because they best or most fully illustrate certain kinds of findings. Unless otherwise noted, therefore, it should be assumed that one study's findings did not contradict another study's conclusions.

It should also be noted that two major studies—in Boston and in Nashville—have so far been minimally referred to. This is because of their somewhat broader frames of reference. The Boston study's focus involved both significant historical perspectives and analytical concerns with effects on the local political system.[18] The Nashville study's emphasis was also more city-wide—it examined the *process* whereby citizen groups became involved with politics and the administrative machinery of local government.[19] Both studies, therefore, have a more direct relevance to the larger question of how citizen participation fits into the basic political framework of city government. To some degree, this is the subject matter of the next, concluding chapter.

NOTES

1. The relative infrequency of and difficulties inherent in analyzing the effects of public programs is well outlined in Joseph S. Wholey, John W. Scanlon, Hugh G. Duffy, James S. Fukumoto and Leona M. Vogt, *Federal Evaluation Policy* Washington, D.C.: The Urban Institute, 1970. Such "relative infrequency" now contrasts more sharply than ever with the rapid development of a broad range of methods and techniques applicable to program evaluation and operational analysis.

2. As previously noted, the establishment of three categories of groups for study, and agreement on issue-analysis methods, constituted the basic parameters of the citizen participation study's general approach. The Atlanta Urban Observatory had initial responsibility for organizing and testing case-study methods, and, as has also been noted, the study group in Kansas City, Kansas took responsibility for developing a scheme for logically classifying citizen groups. There were, therefore, only tacit understandings that study cities would do some inventorying of local groups and would deal with problems of assessing group effectiveness.

3. See Atlanta study report.

4. This outcome was not unique to the Atlanta study. If anything, the relationship between specificity of group demand and organizationally effective outcomes was the most ubiquitous finding across study cities. This represented, therefore, still another apparent affirmation of the Alinsky tenet that groups must focus on issues that are simple, specific, and concrete enough to be communicated. For an analysis of these and related questions, see Charles F. Levine, "Understanding Alinsky: Conservative Wine in Radical Bottles," *American Behavioral Scientist* 17 (November/December 1973): 279–284.

5. See Atlanta study report.

6. See Frank X. Steggert and H. Coleman McGinnis, *Zoning Problems in Atlanta: Two Studies of Policy, Practice and Community Acceptance and Their Problem-Solving Applications* (Atlanta Urban Observatory, Atlanta, 1972).

7. See Atlanta study report. As mentioned earlier in this summary, some study cities probed particular citizen participation questions in greater-than-usual depth. This was the case here, and hence the heavy reliance on material from the Atlanta study report.

8. The assumption here is that any reader with some reasonable familiarity with the citizen participation literature would not be at all surprised by these findings.

9. See Milwaukee study report.

10. See *Organized Citizen Participation in Albuquerque* (Albuquerque Urban Observatory, Albuquerque, 1970). Referred to hereafter as Albuquerque study report.

11. This finding is quite consistent throughout the new citizen participation literature.

12. See San Diego study report.
13. See John D. Hutcheson, Jr. and Frank X. Steggert, *Organized Citizen Participation in Urban Areas* (Center for Research in Social Change, Emory University, Atlanta, 1970).
14. See *Organized Citizen Participation in Boston* (Boston Urban Observatory, Boston, 1971). Referred to hereafter as Boston study report.
15. See *Client Participation in Service Organizations* (Cleveland Urban Observatory, Cleveland, 1971). Referred to hereafter as Cleveland study report.
16. See *Citizen Participation Groups: A Report to the National Urban Observatory* (Kansas City Urban Observatory, Kansas City, Kansas, 1971). Referred to hereafter as Kansas City, Kansas study report.
17. See Baltimore study report.
18. See Boston study report.
19. See Nashville study report.

Chapter Six

The Future of Citizen Participation

UNDERSTANDING THE STUDIES

As Chapter 1 emphasized, differences between study cities were such that it was reasonable to expect some differences in the frequency, character, and styles of organized citizen participation. At the same time, this summary's focus has not been on direct city comparisons. Its emphasis has been on findings applicable to all the cities in the study project. Its intent involved outlining the patterns within which individual cities might establish their particular processes and structures for citizen participation.

The question of who belonged to organized groups with city problem concerns turned out to be simple at some levels and complex at other levels. There were clearly city differences, but most stemmed from a few population characteristics. These involved social class and racial factors as both reflected different kinds of concerns about and attitudes toward city government, and as both were manifested in a city's residential character. In terms, therefore, of a given city's planning, development, and service-delivery activities—within its specific pattern of development—what is important is a more rational, objective, and sophisticated understanding of its very particular citizen mix.

Survey data indicated that citizen trust in city government was likely to be lower where population density and the minority-group population proportion were comparatively high. So one can conclude that cities with concentrated racial or ethnic populations will have services that are not going to be seen as very good. In such cities, confidence in officials may be lower than average. While the trust factor for citizens is related to both class and race characteristics, race seems to be the more significant, and neither is uniformly tied to membership in the citizen groups with which local governments may need to work.

For city officials, the extreme situations should be easy to recognize. In citizen-participation terms, the initial problems can be seen as: (1) adequately *understanding* the "less attractive" extreme groups; and (2) accurately appraising the "middle population" and its relevance to politics and participation. In looking at the organized groups that make up a city's parapolitical structure, it is important to realize that for the more visible citizenry, it is the sense of political efficacy that makes a political difference. There is a relationship between the citizen's belief that his participation makes sense, and whether he will or will not belong to a group with some community-betterment potential. Unfortunately, this relationship is not so straightforward and apparent that this is *all* a city official needs to know.

This is not simply an academic assertion. Consider, for example, the set of variables for two study cities depicted in Table 6-1. In this instance the two study cities involved were very different in population size and proportions of their metropolitan areas. At the same time, their densities and minority-group proportions were not too dissimilar. And as Table 6-1 indicates, the organizational membership rank for each city was comparatively low.

Table 6-1. Group Membership and Related Variables in Two Study Cities

Cities	Organizational Membership Rank	Neighborhood Group Membership Rank	Mean Political Trust Score Rank	Mean Political Efficacy Score Rank
Kansas City, Kansas	10	10	7	1
Milwaukee	9	8	3	2

Source: From Tables 2-6, 2-20, and A-2.

While many other factors are not included here, what is being suggested is that confidence in government (political trust) was relatively high in one instance and relatively low in the other, while citizen attitudes about abilities to affect the political system were comparatively high in both cities. While both cities, therefore, had comparatively few organized citizen groups, the groups they did have were likely to be more actively interested in relating to the governmental structure. In the first instance, more such groups were likely to be less trusting, and higher-trust groups were likely to be more recognizable to city officials. In the second instance, the reverse may well be true: with more groups more trusting, and with this as the norm, less-trusting groups might be more recognizable as deviant in their attitudes toward city government.

Similar examples could be developed using other study cities, but the intent here is to illustrate. Such crude hypotheses indicate the need for much more careful and more multidimensional approaches to analyzing citizen participation in specific cities. In a limited sense, this suggests that study cities need to exploit more fully the attitude survey data they already have as a potentially rich source of information about things relating to citizen participation.[1] In a more general way, this also argues that most cities concerned about citizen participation will have to move from simple universal generalizations to the harder work of more disciplined data-gathering and more careful analysis. Such cities will have to map this problem as carefully as they attempt to rationalize and manage their other activities.

Both survey data and study findings can help in understanding the sharp differences between citizen groups, and here they have some real predictive utilities. It is important to know, for example, that upper-class whites are likely to have membership tendencies and definable views about local government that are *both* differentiated within this class and different from other class-race groups of citizens.[2] While these and similar insights are available to those who want to look carefully enough, the problem of the more middle-of-the-road citizen remains. Here it is at least possible that the actions of government and political leadership will make the difference, if there is an attitudinal tipping point for this part of the city's population.

The study's classification of citizen organizations into federal city, and voluntary groups demonstrated similar predictive values. In terms of what has been—and not necessarily what ought to be—city groups have simply been less frequent, less visible, and less controversial. This situation may, of course, be changing as more cities evidence greater interest in questions of administrative and political decentralization. As the 1973 *Municipal Year Book* indicated, a majority of cities surveyed had made some kind of a decentralization effort involving neighborhood meetings, new complaint-handling machineries, community-wide resident advisory committees, neighborhood councils, or multiservice centers.[3]

Study findings should not, therefore, imply that city groups are unimportant. If anything, it is likely that this particular aspect of organized citizen participation will become critically significant during an era of revenue-sharing and locally initiated, area-wide community planning and development. The project's local studies in Boston (of the Little City Hall program) and in Denver (of citizen participation in the functional areas of employment, economic development, housing, and transportation) evidenced an active concern with this more current dimension of community involvement. The issue-orientation of the national study resulted, however, in more knowledge of federal and voluntary groups. Since these groups are not all going to disappear, and since the basic dynamics of citizen participation are not likely to change in any significant way, one ought to assume that study findings will remain relevant for the immediate years ahead.

With this assumption, therefore, it may be very important to realize that the perceived failures of federal groups—some of which may now be part of a city's more permanent institutional infrastructure—stemmed primarily from the character of the tasks that many had been assigned.[4] As the studies quite consistently established, such inner-city groups have been concerned with global problems of neighborhood transformation, while being located in problem-solving structures where they may have had very little of significance to do. With no independent resources and with memberships that were likely to be both politically dissatisfied and expecting to be able to change things, any conflicts such groups may have engendered seem to be what ought to have been anticipated. There are, of course, many implications here for the next community participation era. As with governmental reorganization more generally, cities are going to have to make careful distinctions between territorial (neighborhood) involvement and functional (problem-oriented) participation.[5]

The citizen participation studies also highlighted the significance of understanding which communities are inevitably going to have politically relevant organized activity. The obvious lesson here—for both federal and voluntary groups—is that community action groups are going to act when there is reason, or they see reason, to do so. For most federal groups and voluntary groups in the inner city, the potential to act is a natural function of location in a redevelopment sector, and the fact of formal existence as a community-concerned association. For voluntary groups in adjacent zones and further removed areas, the most explanatory variable is probably the presence or perception of change. It is obvious that new forms of total community development will among other things, diffuse such change potentials. If so, a concurrent result will be a more homogenized set of citizen participation problems.

And how will such organized citizens behave? As the study's analytical framework outlined, this will depend on what it is trying to accomplish, and in part on how it decides to act. The manner in which it will relate to local government, or any of its elements, will be influenced by past relationships and the way in which its current actions are received by government. While local governments can do little about either group tendencies or past history, they do have some capacity to influence present and future situations. There is, however, no single omnibus formula that will work. Although it requires more anticipatory capacity than most bureaucracies have been willing or able to demonstrate, the need is for a more adaptive response geared to the particulars of a situation. In this sense—if relations with communities are really taken seriously—their citizen participation relationships can be viewed as a practical problem in political calibration.

In addition to requiring more information than most cities have, such flexibility runs counter to the more natural behavior disclosed by the studies. The expected tendency is for public officials to approach the question of citizen participation with a broad bias of some particular kind. Among other things, this will usually involve the twin assumptions that the machinery for citizen contact is in place and that there are appropriate routes that should be followed. In noting this, it should be made quite clear that these are not necessarily the unique perspectives of city officials. If anything, these may still be the basic views of the larger society. For example— as one of the Kerner Commission studies pointed out—just a few years ago a third of the white population in fifteen major cities did not differentiate between riots and various forms of nonviolent protest, and a quarter was even opposed to orderly marches protesting discrimination.[6]

There may be, therefore, limited social pressure for more adaptive responses to concerned citizens who do not in fact have very good or very direct access to government. As the studies suggested, the media may be of limited value to many such groups. The likelihood is that city governments will be left relatively free to make up their own minds about how concerned they should be with various kinds of citizen participation issues.

In doing this, it is possible that those cities that proceed more actively and "progressively" may still overlook groups that are less politically visible. As some of these studies pointed out, community groups that work at their concerns in a quieter and more continuing way may also need and benefit from assistance from local government. In a very real sense, unless these kinds of groups are rediscovered with more areawide community-development activity, they are likely to erode away.

APPLYING THE FINDINGS

Much of the foregoing urges greater diagnostic capacities for cities seriously interested in planning for organized citizen participation. But since participation is usually so broadly defined, this raises the question of how it can be viewed to see the major pieces of the problems. As the Baltimore study noted, there appear to be two major conceptions of citizen participation.[7] The first portrays participation as a means by which citizen desires are communicated to public officials. The second is more concerned about the impact on citizens themselves—the potential of community participation for overcoming the isolation, alienation, and sense of powerlessness that are supposedly characteristics of urbanites, and particularly the urban poor.

As the tone of this analysis should have indicated, the emphasis of the studies was clearly on the first conception. The working assumption has been that citizen participation makes a place in the political system for citizen demands that might otherwise go unstated, unheard, or unanswered. A concurrent assumption has been that government officials then become more acutely conscious of public opinion, and their decisions may more closely reflect what the public wants.[8]

With this frame of reference, it was necessary to fit organized citizen participation to a systematic understanding of the political system. The Atlanta study—the first completed—did this, and most other study cities accepted the model developed for that study. Figure 6-1 reproduces this model.[9]

Although the model may initially appear formidable, it is really not very complex. It indicates that an issue of concern to some citizens arises in the community (the political system's local environment), and that a variety of things will influence *whether, how,* and *when* the concern comes to the attention of government. The issue-concerned group, either ad hoc or already organized, can be the carrier, and it may or may not be able to go directly to government. There may or may not be opposition groups, and the initiating group can be either a support *or* an opposition group. Such issue initiation can also, of course, come from one or more of the community's

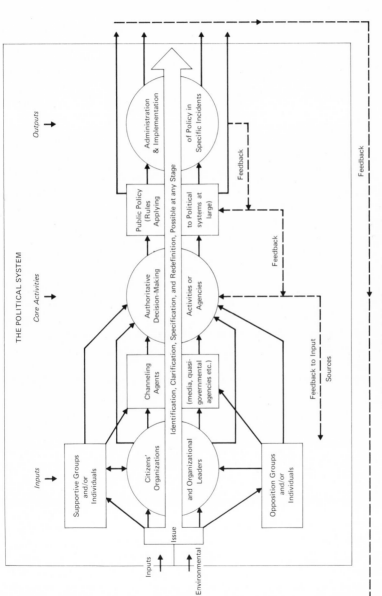

THE POLITICAL SYSTEM

Inputs   Core Activities   Outputs

The Environment of the Political System (other systems)

Source: John D. Hutcheson, Jr. and Frank X. Steggert, *Organized Citizen Participation in Urban Areas* (Atlanta: Center for Research in Social Change, Emory University, 1970), p. 33.

Figure 6-1. Organized Citizen Participation in the Political System

established organizations. In pressing its view of the issue, the group may or may not be able to obtain support from the media or any available quasi-governmental body (e.g., community-relations board, neighborhood center, and so on).

This model suggests that the problem of gaining access to local government in today's larger-scale and more complex world involves much more than a citizen writing to his alderman. If a community issue is of any real social or political consequence, a large array of groups may be competitively clamoring for government's attention. As the model also indicates, an issue—particularly a volatile one—is not a one-time thing. It is likely to undergo many changes (clarifications, specifications, and redefinitions) as it continues to be politically relevant.[10]

This raises at least two sets of questions for local governments. The first is structural, and concerns the kinds of agencies or institutions (private, quasi-governmental, governmental) that exist—or do not exist—as the community's issue-input machinery. The second set of questions is more dynamic, and has to do with the processes available—or not available—for monitoring and negotiating as issues become more politically developed. Most of the citizen participation studies were concerned with these kinds of questions, and their findings can thus contribute to mapping the political system's input terrain.

What the model does not show is the specific character of the political system's environment. Attitude survey data were, therefore, introduced to emphasize the relevance of general political attitudes to the various paths that different citizens groups may take in bringing issues to government. From these data and from study findings, it should be obvious that there is no simple singular thing that local governments can do to handle all of the different politically relevant events that can occur during community-issue formation.

There is a real danger, however, that some cities may shift from the general view that all citizens should approach government in some reasonably uniform way, to the notion that there is a single structural way to link all interested citizens more closely to government operations. Some may opt for public-information meetings, others for new organizational structures, and still others for more public opinion polling. In reality, however, all three strategies are relevant to a political system that wants to be more acutely conscious of citizen attitudes.[11]

One might conceive of a community's citizenry—in an admittedly oversimplified example—as composed of: (1) those who want to know what is going on and want to be kept informed; (2) those who, in addition, want to influence what is further likely to happen, and who want to control events in some rather specific ways; and (3) those who have very minimal interest in public events, and who will remain aloof unless their very personal concerns are likely to be negatively affected. For the first group, public information strategies are likely to be both appropriate and sufficient. They are obviously not enough for citizens in the second category, and here the citizen participation questions in project studies must be dealt with. However, neither strategy will tap the remaining category of less-interested citizens. For these citizens, only survey and other observational kinds of approaches will allow government to assess what their attitudes and wishes may be.[12]

Returning to the model presented in Figure 6-1, one can argue that such emphases are unnecessary—that most citizens are concerned with what local government *does*, or with the city services and other benefits that make up the outputs of the political system. If this is so, then attention and scarce resources should not be diverted to developing machineries that will produce more demands from more and more citizen groups. While there is a logic to such a results-oriented approach, the problems of citizen participation are not that simple. Results *are* important and, with the feedback processes that inhere in any system, the quality of city services will affect the citizen's level of political trust and his support of the political system (an *input* variable).

This will require, however, a more equivalent level of services throughout the community if the political trust levels of citizens are going to be uniformly higher. But while this is necessary, it is not sufficient. As earlier discussion has indicated, the political attitudes of citizens involve other dimensions besides satisfaction with services. Political trust also involves belief in the integrity of officials, and political efficacy implies that at least some citizens feel they should be more involved in community affairs. For these reasons and for these citizens, issues of organized citizen participation continue to be very relevant.

Government's normal response to this kind of argument has been the establishment of citizen advisory groups. As the studies suggested, such governmental groups—primarily the federal groups—have not tended to function very well. They have been generally viewed as unproductive or troublesome. Here again the political-system model has some explanatory power. The citizen advisory group approach tends to see citizen involvement at the *output* end—as providing advice to agencies on policy implementation and program administration matters. In this sense, the citizens involved are somewhat locked into the agency's overall organizational structure. They may, moreover, be located at or near the bottom of the influence chain. If so, decentralization of such citizen groups—as within some federal programs—may make matters worse in further removing such advisors from central decisionmaking.

In the jargon of systems analysis, such government groups are expected to provide "withinputs." Since they are connected with government, they are somehow more *in* the political system, and it does not seem appropriate that they should behave otherwise. In this sense, officials may see such advisory bodies as' different from voluntary groups. The latter are, therefore, more properly in the political system's environment: at or near the input end of the model. As such, their behavior as demand groups is like other established interest groups, and this phenomenon is familiar to most government officials.

ASSESSING THE FUTURE

The emphasis here on understanding the nuances of this particular political-system model comes from the belief that the new era of citizen participation will focus on building "partnerships" with citizens as part of local community development activities. If this prognosis is correct, the political system problems of citizen parti-·cipation discussed in the studies will shift to a new format. In a sense, therefore, such problems will be shoved down to the level of the new and more comprehensively concerned agencies that will likely be established for community planning and development.

Such agencies do, of course, already exist, and a few are actively engaged in trying to fit citizen involvement to community-development processes that are likely, under revenue-sharing, to be more heavily technical. Figure 6-2 diagrams such an approach from a systems engineering point of view. While this diagram represents an idealized perspective and *not* an operational model, it is offered here as one view of a local planning future. As the creator of the model well recognizes, the problem of goal synthesis is critical to the success of applying analytical technologies to the planning process. No solutions are immediately available, and thus problems of community involvement and citizen participation remain basic to the creation of viable planning processes. It should be remembered, of course, that such planning will continue to occur within the community's existing political system.[13]

Similar problems of citizen participation are likely to continue to plague more conventional kinds of planning processes.

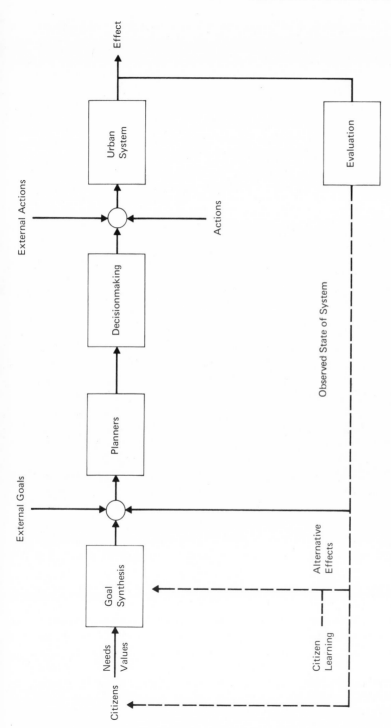

Source: Frank DiCesare, "An Interactive Goal Setting and Planning System for Small Cities," *Proceedings of the 6th Hawaii Conference on Systems Science* (January 1973). Used by Permission.

Figure 6–2. Citizen Involvement in the Community-Development Process

As many analysts have noted, involving citizens in planning results in both costs and benefits.[14] Table 6-2, however, outlines some factors that are likely to lead many local communities in the direction of a partnership model. As this matrix indicates, while the partnership model may ultimately be the more feasible, it does require technical assistance costs in order to obtain positive citizen participation benefits.

Table 6-2. Citizen Participation in the Planning Process

	Costs-Benefits[a]		
Variables	*Community[b] Control Models*	*Consultant/ Advisory[c] Models*	*Partnership[d] Models*
Leadership Development	+	—	+
Efficiency	—	+	0
Resolution of Conflict	+	—	+
Reduction of Promise Delivery-Gap	—	—	+
Costs of Technical Assistance	—	0	—
Effectiveness in Meeting Goals	+	0	+
Sense of Community	+	0	+
Commitment to Programs	+	—	+
Provision of Lay Viewpoints	+	—	+

[a]The plus symbol indicates assumption that a model would positively contribute to an outcome variable; the minus symbol assumes negative contribution; and zero assumes neutral effect. In all instances, values assigned are those to be expected from modal views of officials. It is *their* perceptions that are assumed.
[b]Composite of minus values assumes that these models are more costly, as time-consuming, more requiring of technical support, and less goal-effective because of "unreality" of aspirations.
[c]Single plus value of efficiency is counterbalanced by failure to facilitate (minus values) any major variables associated with active community involvement.
[d]Large number of plus values assumes that partnership, with technical support and additional consumption of time can incorporate plus values of community-control models.
Source: Adapted from the literature by Carl A. Ruppert, Program in Public Management, Rensselaer Polytechnic Institute. Used by permission.

CONCLUSIONS

Applying study findings might require many different adjustments in the local political system. In considering this, however, it is important to realize that many adjustments have already taken place, and more are in process.[15] As mentioned in Chapter 5, both the Boston and Nashville studies were primarily concerned with larger patterns of political change, which organized citizen participation helped bring about.

On the basis of both historical and case-study analysis, the Boston study concluded that recent federally supported citizen participation activities have created new sensitivities among policy-makers that are now an established part of the political scene. Officials are now more alert to perceived neighborhood needs and decentralization options, and a larger number of citizens are now more acquainted with the complexities of planning and resource allocation. In this sense, organized citizen participation has become an additional established input to the traditional political system.[16] One can then argue that, taken collectively, the activities of new citizen participation groups have been effective. The political system has been permanently altered.[17]

As the Boston cases well illustrated, however, both local government and citizen groups have learned to adapt on the basis of many different kinds of accommodation. Major issues have involved conflict *and* collaboration, conflict *and* compromise, and still other types of more specific relationships. In each instance, the ultimate resolution of issues around which citizen groups were very active involved decisions about what was best under the circumstances.[18]

In pursuing similar and related questions, the Nashville study concluded that major community issues take a long time to resolve, and that such issues will evolve through various stages on their way to resolution. This extended issue-handling inevitably involves three elements: (1) political leadership; (2) citizens; and (3) the administrative agencies charged with planning and development responsibilities. Although this study's analysis was very thorough, its essential messages were: (1) the traditional political system can no longer resolve major community issues with established processes and traditional machinery; and (2) new kinds of "high-trust" citizen groups provide the means through which political executives and appointed officials can accomplish the complex tasks of urban redevelopment.[19] For many, this is the overall message of the new citizen participation.

At the same time, local government officials are undoubtedly aware that majority sentiment may support staying with traditional ways of doing things. Although the value of representativeness may not as yet have run its course, the mood of many is for more orderliness and good management.[20] Organized citizen participation may be, therefore, more politically avoidable in at least some situations. Although researchers connected with the citizen participation study have not been polled on the matter, an educated guess would be that they would see such avoidance as very unwise—with the ultimate costs far outweighing any immediate benefits.

FINAL REMARKS

It is customary to begin a manuscript with one or more quotations, presumably to establish the context and to set the tone for what is to come. In this instance, however, it is more appropriate to end with the following somewhat extended statement that appeared in the *New York Times* in mid-1974:

> The most inevitable conclusion is that our cities need some new mechanism by which to rebuild themselves. The old power structure of reform-minded mayors backed by strong chamber of commerce interests served a good purpose at one time: it could make decisions and implement them within a relatively short period.
>
> But the exclusiveness of that alliance has made it obsolete. The cry of the times is for some form of what is optimistically called citizen participation. The problem is how to weld all the voices who rightfully want to participate in their destiny into an action-oriented body.
>
> Effective, broad-based local participation is crucial because rebuilding a city is not a program like getting to the moon. There are, after all, no people on the moon. Only the local leaders are close enough to understand the most important aspect of a city: its human component.
>
> This doesn't mean we don't need Federal help, lots of it, in terms of dollars. But I would like to see Federal programs initiated and shaped by city leaders—and their constituencies—who will implement them. In the final analysis only they can be held responsible.[21]

To some degree, this represents the increasingly frequent perception that cities, particularly those that are no longer growing, may be facing still another crisis—this time a citizen crisis. A set of dilemmas persists. As city problems continue, the exit-prone who have the means will continue to leave. Those with means who want to stay can only become disillusioned if problems continue and local government fails to respond. As they, in turn, exit, the city is left with those who have only voice, and even their voices can ultimately lapse into passivity. Can really viable forms of citizen participation, together with resources, break the cycle? This may well be the critical urban question of the seventies.

NOTES

1. For an analysis relating survey data to citizen participation questions in a study city (Milwaukee), see Peter K. Eisinger, "The Urban Crisis as a Failure of Community," *Urban Affairs Quarterly* 9, (June 1974), 437–461.

2. See, for example, Table A-10, with its attendant inferences.

3. See the analysis in Carl W. Stenberg, *The New Grass Roots Government?* (Advisory Commission on Intergovernmental Relations, Washington, 1972).

4. As this is written, the continuity of the community-action agencies established under the Economic Opportunity Act is still somewhat tentative. Although legislation establishing the Community Services Administration as a new funding source will keep such agencies viable for the immediate future, their longer term existence is less certain. Without further enabling legislation, the continued (and continuing) existence of these local agencies becomes an empirical question. One might speculate that those (relatively few) that would survive under such circumstances would be either (1) those that had developed to a stage where their functional relationships with local governments were cooperatively viable; or (2) those that had developed such political influence that they could not be readily dispensed with.

5. Within the former (territorial or neighborhood involvement), critical questions of the degree and character of administrative or political decentralization remain. These and related questions are discussed in the Boston "local agenda" report on that city's Little City Hall program. For a more detailed analysis, see Eric A. Nordlinger and Jim Hardy, "Urban Decentralization: An Evaluation of Four Models," *Public Policy* 20 (Summer 1972): 359-396.

6. For these and related questions, see Angus Campbell and Howard Schuman, *Racial Attitudes in Fifteen American Cities* (Survey Research Center, University of Michigan, Ann Arbor, 1968).

7. See Baltimore study report.

8. The studies were thus more or less automatically accepting of the traditional "group model" in public policy analysis. For an introductory discussion of this and other complementing or competitive models, see Thomas R. Dye, *Understanding Public Policy*, 2nd ed. (New York: Prentice-Hall, 1975).

9. The model derives from the general analysis of David Easton in *The Political System* (New York: Knopf, 1959).

10. As previously alluded to, this was one of the major conclusions of the Nashville citizen participation study, with additional more specific conclusions of an organizational or structural kind. See Nashville study report.

11. As the Jackson/Slade reference in Chapter 4 noted, "citizen participants" and the "community at large" are likely to have quite different perceptions of the city as a social-change agent. In the course of applying Hirschman's exit and voice options at the neighborhood-analysis level, Orbell and Uno demonstrate a broad range of differential perceptions between those who are voice-prone—and thus much more likely to be politically active—and those who are not. See John M. Orbell and Toru Uno, "A Theory of Neighborhood Problem Solving: Political Action vs. Residential Mobility,"

American Political Science Review 66 (June 1972): 471–489.

12. Recent publications of the Urban Institute and articles in the journal literature are increasingly suggesting that such a survey focus on the part of city governments is both desirable and feasible.

13. The prognosis does not depict what is likely to be an immediate future situation. As presently available data on general revenue-sharing experience indicates, the immediate impact of such funds is in the direction of more of the same. For a description and analysis of this question, see the 1974 *Municipal Year Book* article, "General Revenue Sharing: Initial Decisions," by David A. Caputo and Richard L. Cole. In citizen-participation terms, the analysis suggests that "most cities are not and probably will not use revenue-sharing funds to supplement or to replace categorical grant programs such as urban renewal, community action, or model cities." The reference here is, of course, to the use of general revenue-sharing funds. Additional data suggest that nearly half of the cities sampled did not hold public hearings prior to their initial revenue sharing decisions; that mayor-council cities were the least likely to have held such hearings; and that the more partisan and "unreformed" the city, the less is the likelihood for citizen input through public hearings.

14. See, for example, Robert A. Aleshire, "Planning and Citizen Participation," *Urban Affairs Quarterly* 5 (June 1970): 369–393.

15. While one tends to think of New York City and Washington, D.C. in terms of such community-oriented political adjustments, such changes are now much more widely distributed. See, for example, "Part I: Neighborhood Councils in Dayton," in "Dayton's Jim Kunde: A New Breed of City Manager," *Nation's Cities* (September 1973), pp. 32–36. For a provocative analysis of other kinds of recent political adjustments in a study city, see "A New Politics in Atlanta," *The New Yorker* (December 31, 1973), pp. 28–40.

16. See Boston study report.

17. This question was not, unfortunately, attended to in the recent (Winter 1974) special issue of *The Public Interest*—"The Great Society: Lessons for the Future." While a number of the articles involved recognized the citizen participation thrust of the sixties as a significant element, no judgments were rendered. This in itself may be noteworthy.

18. See Boston study report.

19. See Nashville study report.

20. In terms of Kaufman's cycle-of-values theory, the apparent deemphasis of citizen participation in the early seventies can be seen as temporary, with the representativeness value continuing to some degree and potentially reasserting itself in the future. See Herbert Kaufman, "Administrative Decentralization and Political Power," *Public Administration Review* 29 (January-February 1969): 3–15.

21. Andrew Heiskell, "For a New Approach to Rebuilding Cities," *New York Times*, April 20, 1974.

Appendix A

Membership Data from the Citizens' Attitude Survey

The tables included in Chapter 2 are those that either (1) depict relationships that are statistically significant; or (2) contribute in some meaningful way to the chapter's narrative flow. Tables A-1 through A-9 provide supplementary data in support of generalizations in the narrative. Table A-10 and the summary statements following this table are included here because of the length and relative complexity of this material.

Table A–1.   Percentages in Organizations Working on City Problems

	Albuquerque	Atlanta	Baltimore	Boston	Denver	Kansas City, Kansas	Kansas City, Missouri	Milwaukee	Nashville	San Diego
City Population 18 or over (#)	158,863	337,464	602,532	459,266	358,170	108,925	340,917	482,182	301,157	483,427
Members (%)	15.3	19.1	16.6	12.7	15.8	6.2	12.0	8.8	14.9	13.9
Nonmembers (%)	84.7	80.9	83.4	87.3	84.2	93.8	88.0	91.2	85.1	86.1

Source: Original data, Urban Observatory Program's Citizens' Attitude Survey, 1971.

Table A-2.   City Rankings on Adult Populations and Organizational Membership Proportions

City	Adult Population Ranking	Organizational Membership Ranking
Atlanta	7	1
Baltimore	1	2
Denver	5	3
Albuquerque	9	4
Nashville	8	5
San Diego	2	6
Boston	4	7
Kansas City, Missouri	6	8
Milwaukee	3	9
Kansas City, Kansas	10	10

Source: Original data, Urban Observatory Program's Citizens' Attitude Survey, 1971.

Table A-3.   City Rankings on Neighborhood Organization Membership Proportions, Population Densities, and Minority-Group Population Proportions

City	Neighborhood Group Ranking	Population Density Ranking	Black Population Ranking	Spanish Descent Population Ranking
Baltimore	1	2	2	8.5
Boston	2	1	6	5.5
Denver	3	5	8	2
Atlanta	4	8	1	8.5
San Diego	5	9	9	3
Albuquerque	6	6	10	1
Nashville	7	10	4.5	8.5
Milwaukee	8	4	7	8.5
Kansas City, Missouri	9	7	3	4
Kansas City, Kansas	10	3	4.5	5.5

Source: Original data, Urban Observatory Program's Citizens' Attitude Survey, 1971.

Table A-4.   Race and Organizational Membership

Race	Members	Non-Members
Whites[a]	14.46%	85.54%
Blacks[b]	13.37	86.63
Total Survey Group	14.15%	85.85%

[a]Excludes people of Spanish descent.

[b]Includes small numbers of other non-white groups.

Source: Recoded data, Urban Observatory Program's Citizens' Attitude Survey, 1972.

Table A–5. Mean Scores on Political Trust Index in Study Cities

City	Albuquerque	Atlanta	Baltimore	Boston	Denver	Kansas City Kansas	Kansas City Missouri	Milwaukee	Nashville	San Diego
Mean Score	17.09	16.20	14.60	13.93	16.60	15.62	14.74	16.93	15.80	18.01
Rank	2	5	9	10	4	7	8	3	6	1

Source: Recoded data, Urban Observatory Program's Citizens' Attitude Survey, 1972.

Table A–6. Organizational Membership and Average Trust Score Rankings in Study Cities

City	Organizational Membership Rank	Mean Political Trust Score Rank	Neighborhood Group Membership Rank
Atlanta	1	5	4
Baltimore	2	9	1
Denver	3	4	3
Albuquerque	4	2	6
Nashville	5	6	7
San Diego	6	1	5
Boston	7	10	2
Kansas City, Missouri	8	8	9
Milwaukee	9	3	8
Kansas City, Kansas	10	7	10

Source: Recoded data, Urban Observatory Program's Citizens' Attitude Survey, 1972.

Table A–7. Organizational Membership and Levels of Political Trust

Membership Classification	Trust Scores of 6 through 13	Trust Scores of 14 through 17	Trust Scores of 18 through 26
Members	23.0%	37.6%	39.4%
Nonmembers	28.1	36.7	35.2
Total Survey Group	27.5%	36.9%	35.6%

Source: Recoded data, Urban Observatory Program's Citizens' Attitude Survey, 1972.

Table A–8.   Mean Scores on Political Efficacy Index in Study Cities

City	Albuquerque	Atlanta	Baltimore	Boston	Denver	Kansas City, Kansas	Kansas City, Missouri	Milwaukee	Nashville	San Diego
Mean Score	7.98	7.92	8.25	8.10	8.20	8.50	8.06	8.43	8.36	8.2
Rank	9	10	5	7	6	1	8	2	3	4

Source: Recoded data, Urban Observatory Program's Citizens' Attitude Survey, 1972.

Table A-9. Organizational Membership and Levels of Political Efficacy

Membership Classification	Efficacy Scores of 3 through 7	Efficacy Scores of 8 through 9	Efficacy Scores of 10 through 15
Members	25.6%	47.7%	26.7%
Nonmembers	33.2	42.8	24.0
Total Survey Group	32.2%	43.5%	24.3%

Source: Recoded data, Urban Observatory Program's Citizens' Attitude Survey, 1972.

Table A-10. Social Class, Race, and Political Trust—Efficacy Levels

Social Class by Ethnicity	Both Trust and Efficacy High	High Trust and Low Efficacy	Low Trust and High Efficacy	Both Trust and Efficacy Low
White[a] Upper Class	37.5%	28.4%	17.2%	16.9%
Black[b] Upper Class	17.4	23.3	33.7	25.6
White Middle Class	30.8	24.5	21.0	23.7
Black Middle Class	17.8	22.8	27.9	31.5
White Lower Class	22.3	31.2	18.3	28.2
Black Lower Class	16.0	29.7	20.3	34.0
Total Survey Group	27.3%	26.3%	21.2%	25.2%

[a]Excludes people of Spanish descent.

[b]Includes small numbers of other non-white groups.

Source: Recoded data, Urban Observatory Program's Citizens' Attitude Survey, 1972.

SUMMARY STATEMENTS

Removing from consideration *all* citizens whose trust and efficacy views are near-average, a rather sharp definition of race and class differences emerges. These can be summarized as follows:

1. At all class levels, whites are more likely than blacks to have *both* more than average confidence in their local governments and an above-average level of confidence in their abilities to influence city politics. While the proportion of whites who have both kinds of confidence decreases from upper to middle to lower classes, class differences among blacks with both such attitudes are not very great. The frequency of holding both sets of opinions is racially most different at the upper level, and least different among the two lower classes.

2. Of those with above-average trust attitudes and below-average

efficacy feelings, whites at all class levels are somewhat more represented than blacks. The differences on a class basis are not, however, very great—particularly at the middle and lower levels. Within both races, the class pattern is similar. Within every class-race grouping, approximately two to three of those who are non-average reflect this high-trust/low-efficacy pattern.

3. Of those with below-average trust attitudes and above-average feelings of efficacy, blacks at all levels are more confident of being able to exert political influence than whites. This is most apparent at the upper-class level, and least significant among the lower classes. With blacks, the order of frequency is from upper to lower. With whites, this pattern is somewhat more characteristic of the middle class.

4. At all class levels, whites will, less frequently than blacks, reflect below-average trust *and* efficacy views. For both races, the frequency of this set of negative views increases as one moves from upper to lower classes.

5. For whites with nonaverage attitudes, upper- and middle-class groups are similar in that proportions move from high trust and efficacy to high trust and low efficacy to low trust and high efficacy. More middle- than upper-class whites exhibit both kinds of negative perspectives. Lower-class whites depart from the generally common pattern in reflecting more negative views of political efficacy.

6. For blacks with nonaverage attitudes, upper- and middle-class groups are similar in that proportions move from low trust and high efficacy to high trust and low efficacy to high trust and efficacy. As with whites, more middle- than upper-class blacks exhibit both kinds of negative perspectives. Lower-class blacks— again like lower-class whites—depart from the general pattern with more negative views of political efficacy.

Appendix B

The Urban Observatory Program's Citizen Participation Studies

THE INDIVIDUAL CITY STUDIES

All of the completed reports and available publications that might properly be considered as relating to the Urban Observatory Program's Study of Organized Citizen Participation are listed below on a city-by-city basis.

Albuquerque. The Albuquerque citizen participation study is reported in a single volume: *Organized Citizen Participation in Albuquerque* (Albuquerque Urban Observatory, December 31, 1970). Principal investigator and report author was Hiram M. Shaw, then Assistant Director of the Albuquerque Urban Observatory and more recently Deputy Director for Governmental Management, Ohio Commission on Local Government Services.

Atlanta. The primary results of the Atlanta citizen participation study are described in a monograph published by Emory University's Center for Research in Social Change: *Organized Citizen Participation in Urban Areas* (Center for Research in Social Change, Emory University, Atlanta, 1970). Study directors and co-authors of this final report version were John D. Hutcheson, Jr., then Assistant Director of Emory University's Center for Research in Social Change and now Assistant Professor of Urban Life at Georgia State University, and Frank X. Steggert, then Director of the Atlanta Urban Observatory and presently Professor of Public Management at Rensselaer Polytechnic Institute. As the following section indicates, this report is also available through the National Technical Information Service (NTIS). Some additional findings from the Atlanta study are detailed in *General Survey of Organized Citizen Participation* (Atlanta Urban Observatory, July 15, 1970). Frank X. Steggert was the principal author of this interim report.

Baltimore. Basic findings and recommendations from the Baltimore study are summarized in a single volume: *Survey of Organized Citizen Participation in Baltimore* (Baltimore Urban Observatory, 1971). The principal research investigator and author of this study's final report was Matthew Crenson, Department of Political Science, The Johns Hopkins University.

Boston. The Boston Urban Observatory's investigations of citizen participation involved a "national agenda" study paralleling the efforts of other Urban Observatories, and a local agenda analysis of Boston's Little City Halls. The final report of the national agenda study, *Organized Citizen Participation in Boston* (Boston Urban Observatory, October 1971) was prepared by Morton Rubin, Associate Professor of Sociology at Northeastern University. The local agenda study report, *Decentralizing the American City: A Study of Boston's Little City Halls* (Boston Urban Observatory, April 1972) was prepared by Eric A. Nordlinger of Brown University's Department of Political Science. This latter report has also been published by the M.I.T. Press. For this version, see Eric A. Nordlinger, *Decentralizing the City: A Study of Boston's Little City Halls* (Cambridge, Mass.: The M.I.T. Press, 1972).

Cleveland. The Cleveland study's findings are available in a single final report: *Client Participation in Service Organizations* (Cleveland Urban Observatory and Institute of Urban Studies, Cleveland State University, September 1971). Report authors were Roberta Steinbacher and Phyllis Solomon, then Associate Director and Research Associate, respectively, at Cleveland State University's Institute of Urban Studies.

Denver. The Denver Urban Observatory's studies—two national agenda and two local agenda projects—are reported in four volumes under the general title of *Citizen Participation in Denver.* The report of the most general national agenda study, Volume III, *Citizen Power and Participation—Groups, Issues and Impact—Within the Political Culture of Denver* (Denver Urban Observatory, February 1972), was authored by William O. Winter, Professor of Political

Science, and James Adams, Research Associate, at the University of Colorado. The second national agenda study report Volume II, *Citizen Participation as Planned Change: The Auraria Higher Education Center* (Denver Urban Observatory, February 1972), is the work of M. Jay Crowe, Associate Professor of Sociology, and T. Michael Smith, Research Associate, both of the University of Colorado. The initial local agenda investigation, Volume I, *Model Cities and Resident Participation* (Denver Urban Observatory, June 1971), was accomplished by Gresham M. Sykes, Professor of Sociology and Law, and Kyle B. White, Research Associate, of the University of Denver. The second local agenda study, Volume IV, *Citizen Participation in the Systems of Housing, Employment, Transportation, and Economic Development* (Denver Urban Observatory, July 1972), was coordinated by Alfred A. Fothergill, then Professor of Law at the University of Denver and later a staff member of the Idaho Department of Special Services. Contributing authors responsible for subreports included, in addition to Mr. Fothergill: Dwayne C. Nuzum, then Dean of the University of Colorado's College of Environmental Design; Martin L. Moody, Associate Chairman of the University of Colorado's Department of Civil and Environmental Engineering; and Paul G. Graves, Director of the Division of Social Sciences, Community College of Denver.

Kansas City. The Kansas City, Kansas segment of the Mid-America Urban Observatory's study of organized citizen participation is summarized in *Citizen Participation Groups: A Report to the National Urban Observatory* (Urban Studies Group, University of Kansas, 1970). The student group formed for this study element was directed by Forrest J. Berghorn, then Associate Professor of American Studies at the University of Kansas. The Kansas City, Missouri segment is reported in *Organized Citizen Participation in Kansas City, Missouri* (University of Missouri—Kansas City, January 1971). Project director for the Missouri study was Gerhard W. Ditz, Professor of Sociology at the University of Kansas City—Missouri.

Milwaukee. The Milwaukee study project—reporting on issues and groups surveyed in 1969—is summarized in a single final report: *Citizen Participation: Issues and Groups* (Milwaukee Urban Observatory, Spring 1972). Project director and author of the final report was Miriam G. Palay, Assistant Director of the Milwaukee Urban Observatory.

Nashville. The Nashville Urban Observatory's detailed analysis of citizen participation is reported on in *Beyond the Ballot:*

Citizen Participation in Metropolitan Nashville (Bureau of Public Administration, University of Tennessee, 1971). Principal investigators and report authors of the Nashville study were Charles A. Zuzak, now Chairman of Arts and Sciences at the University of Tennessee at Nashville, Kenneth E. McNeil, formerly at Vanderbilt University and currently Assistant Professor of Sociology at the University of Wisconsin, and Frederic Bergerson, formerly at Vanderbilt University and subsequently Instructor in Political Science at Whittier College.

San Diego. The report of the San Diego inquiry into organized citizen participation, *Citizen Participation Groups in San Diego* (The Urban Observatory of San Diego, 1971), was prepared by Frank Barnett, Peter Black, Eleanor Gerber, and Joyce Joseph, graduate students at the University of California at San Diego. The project was directed by Marc J. Swartz, Professor of Anthropology at that institution.

AVAILABILITY OF STUDY REPORTS

The Albuquerque report, the primary Atlanta report, the Boston national agenda study report, the Cleveland report, Volumes I, II, III, and IV of the Denver study, both segments of the Mid-America Urban Observatory's study, the Milwaukee report, the Nashville report, and the San Diego report are presently available through the National Technical Information Service, 5285 Port Royal Road, Springfield, Virginia 22151.

Copies are available in paper and microfiche. Requests for NTIS reports should include the following information:

Title	*Accession No.*		*Price*
Organized Citizen Participation in Albuquerque	PB– 206– 091	Paper Copy Microfiche	$3.00 $1.45
Organized Citizen Participation in Urban Areas [Atlanta study]	PB– 207– 515	Paper Copy Microfiche	$6.75 $1.45
Organized Citizen Participation in Boston	PB– 206– 369	Paper Copy Microfiche	$6.75 $1.45
Client Participation in Service Organizations [Cleveland study]	PB– 207– 042	Paper Copy Microfiche	$3.00 $1.45

Citizen Participation in Denver Volume I	PB- 206- 995	Paper Copy Microfiche	$3.00 $1.45
Citizen Participation in Denver Volume II	PB- 212- 557	Paper Copy Microfiche	$3.00 $1.45
Citizen Participation in Denver Volume III	PB- 208- 341	Paper Copy Microfiche	$3.00 $1.45
Citizen Participation in Denver Volume IV	PB- 214- 388	Paper Copy Microfiche	$3.00 $1.45
Citizen Participation Groups: A Report to the National Urban Observatory [Kansas City, Kansas study]	PB- 206- 994	Paper Copy Microfiche	$3.00 $1.45
Organized Citizen Participation in Kansas City, Missouri *index*	PB- 211- 313	Paper Copy Microfiche	$3.00 $1.45
Citizen Participation: Issues and Groups, Milwaukee Wisconsin, 1969	PB- 213- 107	Paper Copy Microfiche	$3.00 $1.45
Beyond the Ballot: Organized Citizen Participation in Metropolitan Nashville	PB- 213- 635	Paper Copy Microfiche	$6.00 $1.45
Citizen Participation Groups in San Diego	PB- 208- 002	Paper Copy Microfiche	$3.00 $1.45

FRAGMENTS FROM THE STUDIES

As indicated in Chapter 1, the series of city-by-city statements that follows is designed to provide some sense of what significant parts (and major emphases) of individual city studies were all about. Once again, these fragments should not be viewed as summaries. These statements have been deliberately phrased and sequenced to produce a composite narrative that would provide another summary of the overall Citizen Participation Project's findings. Orthodox summaries or abstracts are included in the NTIS reports listed in the preceding section.

The study in Albuquerque assumed that citizen participation as a form of organized social action is now a political fact of life.

In paying attention to the practical aspects of such activity, it looked at groups that had been directly involved with city government. Citizen group action was more effective when it involved cooperation strategies rather than conflict tactics. Public officials favored groups with something to offer; accepted those seeking government sponsorship for their interests; and least preferred those that were likely to create some kind of an impasse situation. The most resolvable kind of issue involved a citizen group with some economic and political resources and a history of negotiating success, and a situation where both parties could benefit.

But protest tactics are not always ineffective. Part of the Atlanta study analyzed two voluntary groups involved in housing controversies. One group was clearly more effective than the other. This more successful group found that protest can be converted into a political resource when the necessary ingredients are present. For a relatively powerless group—with lower-class members, limited membership participation, and few internal resources—this may involve publicity and, more importantly, the support of a third-party organization with community stature and some political access. In such instances protest may be more effective than middle-class "talking activities." Local governments might help, therefore, by sponsoring more community bodies that can act as third-party support organizations.

What city governments do can significantly influence the effectiveness of citizen organizations. The Baltimore study—comparative case studies of representative community groups—identified the "empty agenda" as a critical variable. The study concludes that "the most troublesome deficiency from which a community group can suffer is to have few specific items of business about which to make decisions." Government-sponsored groups are usually part of an effort to achieve general, long-range, and sometimes ill-defined goals, and thus they tend to suffer from empty-agenda kinds of problems. On the other hand, government-provided city planners, as problem-oriented professionals, can help to overcome this situation "by providing groups with significant things to make decisions about."

In order to achieve more difficult or longer-term objectives, groups may need still other forms of assistance. The Boston study recognized this in focusing its analysis on conditions that move organizations to seek partnerships. In this frame of reference, successful group activity is seen as primarily conservative and developmental, rather than radical or revolutionary. Instead of an all-or-nothing situation, such success is likely to involve a continuous process of building coalitions around issues. Unlike the territorially based participation fostered by federal guidelines, this involves much more in the way of broadly based task force activity. In Boston, the trend of the seventies indicates a shift from community coordination and planning activities to more direct political action.

And yet in today's world, with its many decentralizing concerns, more localized kinds of problems are likely to persist. The Cleveland study reflected this in restricting its attention to a single relatively stable black community without any federal program involvement. A focus on client participation in service organizations revealed a bloc of critical problems. Apart from the fact that none of the groups could do anything about either community decay or community improvement, problems of client involvement were formidable. With transitional areas in the community, participation was more individualized and more typical of homeowners and longer-term residents. As far as service agencies were concerned, residents were more aware of those that functioned as multiservice organizations.

Such territorially concerned citizen organizations are likely to increase in most large American cities. Among other things, the Denver study included careful demographic analysis of citizen participation—of both voting behavior and group activity. According to this analysis, the electoral process may now be so vague that it simply excludes many people whose problems do not appear on the ballot. This is probably contributing to more in the way of veto-oriented group protest activity. In any event, the middle-class sectors of the city have demonstrated heightened group action during the past decade. Although this city's area-concerned groups are mainly middle-class, minority-group activity has also increased. This suggests a growing political sophistication contributing to formation of coherent, permanent organizations.

It is not very easy, however, for minority groups to feel successful. In analyzing the characteristics and activities of a broad range of community development organizations, the study in Kansas City, Kansas concluded that income and education levels of group members are the most useful factors in predicting organizational success. In what is described as a "stereotype of the American inner city," in stark contrast to the suburban affluence of parts of the metropolitan area, inner-city groups seem almost bound to fail. As inner-city people with low incomes and lesser degrees of education, they tend to have direct economic concerns—the kind that are least likely to be readily realized. It is not surprising, therefore, that they evoke a relatively limited response from their target bodies.

Problems of inner-city groups may be further complicated

by the fact that both community knowledgeables and the media tend to focus on city issues. In developing this theme, the study in Kansas City, Missouri argues that officials and other knowledgeable observers disagree with newspapers on what the important issues are and which citizen groups are most relevant. Private voluntary groups— older and more stable, self-funding, and with less rank-and-file apathy—may have some capacity to overcome this disability. As middle-class organizations, their members have a greater degree of opportunity to interact with public officials. Inner-city groups— with lower-class membership structures and their usual dependency on government subsidies—confront a very different kind of situation.

City officials do, of course, frequently call on citizen groups for advice or assistance. In discussing this factor and related attitudes toward citizen group activity, the Milwaukee study notes that such self-initiating behavior typically involves prestigious, long-established, business, labor, or church-related organizations. When neighborhood, ethnic, or similar grass-roots organizations are named as contacts, such groups are usually identified by appointed, not elected, officials. Elected and appointed officials are, however, likely to agree on the relative importance of group opinion. Elected officials rank group opinion as less important than agency objectives and agency staff views. Appointed officials rank such opinion as less significant than federal guidelines and staff views.

Involvement of citizen groups with city government can reflect very extended relationships when major issues of urban development are at stake. In tying together a number of metropolitan crisis cases, the Nashville study outlines a process whereby citizen participation develops. Within this process, critical relationships among planning, electoral politics, and citizen support for administrative policies shift with each stage. When traditional political mechanisms fail to resolve the policy questions involved, participation tends to crystallize in a new arena where citizen participation seems inevitable and the outcome will not fit any ideal solution. Timing and skilled and well-informed citizen leaders are then critical factors in reaching cooperative settlements.

When issues are more community-oriented, the normal tendency may be to attempt a closed approach to citizen group involvement. The San Diego study suggests that city officials will want to work closely with one group in the community, usually an established group, on the conservative side, and one that city officials have previously dealt with. It may also be a group with structural ties to local government. This group's ability to function effectively involves keeping conflicting opinions from becoming publicly known, and gathering support through leaders' abilities to communicate with other groups. If open conflict breaks out, it will be harder to obtain official decisions, and nondecisions are more probable. In cases like this, the tone (as well as the character of a group's demands) is important.

City governments do not engage exclusively in avoidance behavior. As the local Boston study suggests, an innovative city government can attempt closer and more continuous contacts with citizens at the neighborhood level—in this case through the Little City Hall approach. This city's program attempts both political and administrative decentralization as a means of effecting better local relationships with service-delivering agencies of city government. In this sense, its ultimate success may hinge on changes in the city's civil service system. After three years, the program can be rated as successful in terms of citizen acceptance. Although the program does not assume dramatic improvement in city services, service deliveries have been significantly upgraded in some of the city's communities.

ADDITIONAL RELATED STUDIES

During the early part of 1974, the National League of Cities reported once again to the Department of Housing and Urban Development on the history, accomplishments, and problems of the Urban Observatory Program. As one subsection of this report indicates, cities in the original network continue to be interested in citizen involvement matters. This continuing interest is evidenced in completed, on-going, or proposed studies of majority-minority attitudes (Denver Urban Observatory), the ombudsman concept in a city government context (Milwaukee Urban Observatory), and alternative structures for community participation (Atlanta Urban Observatory).

Appendix C

Guide to Selected Bibliographies

The available literature on the many different aspects that make up organized citizen participation is voluminous. It is an enormously large and ever-growing literature. This appendix identifies and briefly describes a number of bibliographic sources that subsume many references to subject matters germane to the Urban Observatory Program's Study of Organized Citizen Participation.

CITIZEN PARTICIPATION STUDY BIBLIOGRAPHIES

As a first-stage activity in its citizen participation inquiry, the study team in Kansas City, Kansas developed a cross-indexed bibliography of books (152 references), government publications (20 references), general media items (24 references), unpublished papers and reports (13 references) and journal articles (108 references). These references reflect the citizen participation literature consulted in developing the conceptual outline illustrated and briefly described in Chapter 3 of this book. Index items, in relation to the bibliography, reflect names of authors, names of citizen participation groups, geographical locations of groups, and target conditions and instrumentalities (terms within the conceptual design) of groups. This cross-indexed bibliography is on pages 94 through 134 of the Appendix of *Citizen Participation Groups: A Report to the National Urban Observatory* (Kansas City Urban Observatory, Kansas City, Kansas, 1971).

In a concurrent manner, study personnel in Atlanta developed a topically arranged bibliography from their fairly extensive

103

literature analysis. This topical arrangement resulted in *a section on organized citizen participation in perspective* (272 references), with subsections on "access to influence in the decisionmaking process" (69 references), "methods of access" (78 references, with 7 voting references, 13 interest and pressure-group references, and 58 references to direct participation in decisionmaking), and "access to influence in mass society" (125 references, with 27 references to problems of access in mass society, and 98 references to innovative methods of access); *a section on types of organized citizen participation* (77 references), with subsections on "types of organizations" (18 references), and typology of organized citizen participation" (59 references); *a section on general studies pertaining to organized citizen participation* (113 references), with subsections on "general works" (63 references), "federally initiated organized citizen participation" (30 references), "organized citizen participation initiated by local governments" (7 references), and "voluntary organized citizen participation" (13 references); *a section on case studies of organized citizen participation* (75 references), with subsections on "federally initiated citizen participation" (33 references), "citizen participation initiated by local government" (17 references), and "voluntary citizen participation (25 references); *a section on comparative case studies of organized citizen participation* (22 references), with subsections on "federally initiated citizen participation (10 references), "citizen participation initiated by local government" (2 references), and "voluntary citizen participation" (10 references); and *a section on general biliographic references* (5 references). This topical bibliography is on pages 139–172 of *Organized Citizen Participation in Urban Areas* (Atlanta Urban Observatory, Atlanta, 1971).

OTHER SOURCES

One of the more frequently cited references—included in the final section of the preceding Atlanta study bibliography—is Vincent Mathews, *Citizen Participation: An Analytical Study of the Literature*, Community Relations Service, U.S. Department of Justice, Washington, D.C., 1968.

For a more current and functionally organized reference, the best available source is probably "Bibliography on Citizen Participation" (Appendix A) in Robert K. Yin, William A. Lucas, Peter L. Szanton, and James A. Spindler, *Citizen Participation in DHEW Programs* (Santa Monica, California: The Rand Corporation, January 1973, R–1196–HEW[Draft]). In addition to detailed abstracts of twenty major works considered by the authors as of unusual quality or influence, this bibliography provides references for: (1) citizen participation and health; (2) citizen participation and education: (3) citizen participation and social services; (4) citizen participation and planning; (5) citizen participation in relation to poverty and urban development, (6) volunteers and voluntary organizations; (7) community and neighborhood participation—general; (8) citizen participation—general, theoretical, and other works; (9) works closely associated with citizen participation; and (10) selected bibliographies. As far as subject matters of the Urban Observatory Program's citizen participation study are concerned, sections 4, 5, 6, and 7 are most relevant.

About the Author

Dr. Frank X. Steggert is currently Professor of Public Management at Rensselaer Polytechnic Institute and a faculty member of the Institute's Center for Urban and Environmental Studies. He has previously taught at Georgia State University, the University of New Mexico, the University of Wisconsin, the University of Chicago and Loyola University of Chicago. During 1969-71 he was Director of the Atlanta Urban Observatory. Dr. Steggert has also served as Executive Director of Milwaukee's Community Action and Model Cities Programs, and as Director of Social Planning for the Metropolitan Area Planning Committee of Halifax, Nova Scotia.